SCHOLASTIC

QAR Comprehension Lessons

Grades 6–8

Jacquelin H. Carroll,
Taffy E. Raphael, and
Kathryn H. Au

New York • Toronto • London • Auckland • Sydney
Mexico City • New Delhi • Hong Kong • Buenos Aires

Teaching *Resources*

We appreciate the hard work and contributions of Kari Corsi, Elizabeth Strode, Amy Waechter-Versaw, and Jo Parker to the process of creating the QAR Comprehension Lessons series. We also thank Sarah Glasscock for her stellar editorial work.

Taffy Raphael and Kathy Au
May 2011

Development Editor: Sarah Longhi

Editor: Sarah Glasscock

Copy editor: David Klein

Cover designer: Maria Lilja

Cover photography: © Photodisc

Interior designer: Melinda Belter

Interior illustrations: Robert Squier

ISBN: 978-0-545-26411-2

Copyright © 2011 by Taffy E Raphael and Kathryn H. Au

Contents

Introduction

BY TAFFY E. RAPHAEL AND KATHRYN H. AU

QAR—Question Answer Relationships—is a categorization system detailing the relationship among a question, the text to which the question refers, and the reader's knowledge base. It can serve as a framework for comprehension instruction, as well as a pedagogical tool for improving teachers' and students' questioning abilities.

The *QAR Comprehension Lessons* books are designed to support teachers who wish to improve comprehension instruction in their classroom, teams of teachers within grade levels or departments who wish to build coherence into their comprehension instruction, and school staff members who are developing a coherent staircase comprehension curriculum. Current initiatives, such as widespread adoption of the Common Core State Standards, emphasize comprehension in learning across the disciplines and highlight the importance of helping all students reach high levels of achievement. Yet teaching comprehension and critical thinking about text, the *raison d'être* for reading, has challenged literacy educators for decades.

Although comprehension is one of the most critical outcomes for literacy instruction, teachers and students can't see, touch, or examine it directly. Comprehension is famously elusive, and our goal in these books is to demystify its instruction.

Comprehension Strategies

Readers use an array of comprehension strategies to construct the author's intended meaning (see Israel & Duffy, 2009). But which comprehension strategies should teachers focus on? Table 1 details similarities and variations in how comprehension has been described in widely cited reviews of research (e.g., Dole, Duffy, Roehler, & Pearson, 1991) and popular professional literature (e.g., Fountas & Pinnell, 2001; Hoyt, 2005). Our understanding of the research led us to emphasize the six strategies shown in Table 1.

In *QAR Comprehension Lessons*, we teach routines to support comprehension through predicting, drawing inferences, identifying important information, summarizing, questioning, and monitoring. Despite slight variations in the way researchers have categorized comprehension strategies, these strategies and our approach to teaching them (see Au & Raphael, 2010; Raphael, & Au, in press; Raphael et al., 2009) align with those of other contemporary literacy educators and researchers (e.g., Dole et al., 1991; Fountas & Pinnell, 2001; Harvey & Goudvis, 2007; Hoyt, 2005; McLaughlin & Allen, 2009).

TABLE 1   **A Comparison of Comprehension Categories**

QAR STRATEGY FOCUS	DOLE ET AL. (1991)	FOUNTAS & PINNELL (2001)	HOYT (2005)	HARVEY & GOUDVIS (2007)	MCLAUGHLIN & ALLEN (2009)
Predicting		Predicting	Predicting Creating images	Activating background knowledge Visualizing	Predicting Previewing Visualizing
Drawing Inferences	Drawing Inferences Predicting	Inferring Connecting Analyzing Critiquing	Inferring Connecting Using analogy	Making Inferences Visualizing	Inferring Visualizing
Identifying Important Information	Identifying Important Information	Gathering	Determining Importance Skimming Scanning		Identifying
Summarizing	Summarizing	Summarizing Synthesizing	Summarizing Paraphrasing Comparing	Synthesizing	Reconstructing
Questioning	Questioning		Self-Questioning		Self-Questioning
Monitoring	Monitoring	Monitoring			Evaluating Judging

Table 2 provides what we regard as reasonable definitions and purposes for these strategies, and their relationship to specific QARs.

TABLE 2   **Defining Comprehension Strategies**

QAR	COMPREHENSION STRATEGY	DEFINITION
Author & Me	Predicting	Using text information and background knowledge and experience to create a hypothesis that anticipates what is going to occur in the text
Author & Me	Drawing Inferences	Constructing ideas and interpretations using information that is not explicitly stated in the text
Right There * Think & Search	Identifying Important Information	Sorting the essential from non-essential content to achieve the purpose(s) for reading
Right There * Think & Search	Summarizing	Creating a brief, coherent text from the essential content of the original source
Author & Me	Questioning	Raising and responding to queries whether explicit or implied
Author & Me	Monitoring	Being aware of the quality and degree of understanding and knowing how to address comprehension breakdowns

The content, structure, and format of the lessons presented in this book reflect four fundamental elements.

1. Comprehension instruction begins with the building of a shared language for discussing comprehension strategies and challenges.

2. Lessons are framed in terms of the reading cycle that reflects readers' stances before, during, and after reading.

3. Specific comprehension strategies or combinations of strategies are taught within the context of the reading cycle, using the language of QAR.

4. Lessons across the three books (grades 2–3, grades 4–5, grades 6–8) are parallel. For example, Lesson 14 always focuses on questioning with narrative text. However, the routines and tools taught within the lesson reflect a developmental approach to curriculum, with texts becoming more challenging, and strategies more sophisticated, as students move up the grades.

QAR: A Shared Language
for Comprehension Instruction

A shared language for discussing the information sources used to construct meaning is central to the *QAR Comprehension Lessons* books. QAR provides the shared language to be used by both teachers and students. As a shared language, QAR can connect strategy instruction across content areas within a classroom, classrooms within a grade level, and grade levels across a whole school (Raphael, Highfield, & Au, 2006). It gives teachers greater precision in conveying complex concepts associated with comprehension, such as where knowledge comes from; relationships among questions or purposes for reading, text, and readers' knowledge; and relationships among strategies and their use across the curriculum. The QAR language also gives teachers a means to model and think aloud about comprehension with their students. Once students learn the language of QAR, they are better able to describe and discuss the comprehension problems they are encountering.

Learning the four core QARs is a first step for teachers and students. But the value of QAR comes from students and teachers using its language to explain their thinking while working to comprehend text. Since questions are central to establishing purposes for engaging with all kinds of text, the vocabulary helps teachers and students communicate about questions (i.e., purposes for reading) and their relationship to various sources of information. It guides them in determining the most useful or appropriate sources of information for accessing or constructing answers to the questions. Figure 1 displays the basic vocabulary of QAR, which consists of three paired comparisons. This vocabulary remains consistent regardless of students' age levels, reading abilities, or dispositions.

FIGURE 1

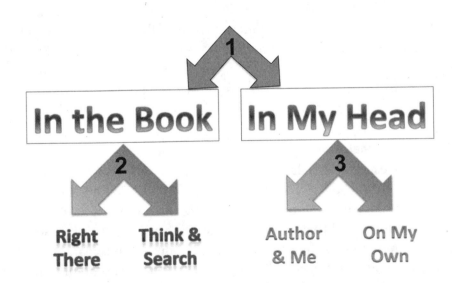

The First Paired Comparison:
In the Book/In My Head

The first paired comparison introduces students to the metaphors of "head" and "book." The terms distinguish between information external to the text source (*In My Head*) or internal to the text source (*In the Book*). The term *head* refers to the reader's knowledge and life experiences (i.e., prior or background knowledge). The term *book* stands for all kinds of texts: conventional print materials, including books, magazines, and newspapers; digital formats such as Web pages and blogs; and graphic images, including charts, graphs, and video. Evidence of learning can be seen when new In the Book information acquired today becomes In My Head background information tomorrow. With these broad distinctions in mind, think about the information sources needed to answer each of the following questions about a story that describes a highly unusual set of events at a youngster's birthday party:

▷ What is the most unusual birthday party you've ever attended?

▷ What were the things about Ellie's birthday party that surprised Nate?

The first question does not require readers to have understood the story or even to have read it. There are many possible answers since readers likely have a range of birthday party experiences and different criteria for what constitutes "unusual." In contrast, to answer the second question, readers must understand sufficient information from the text to distinguish unexpected from expected features of the party. The first question is an In My Head QAR; the second, an In the Book (Raphael et al., 2006; Raphael & Au, in press).

The Second Paired Comparison:
Right There/Think & Search

The second paired comparison distinguishes between the two In the Book QARs: Right There and Think & Search. These QARs differ in terms of the *place(s)* in the text in which students can find relevant information for answering the question. With Right There QARs, all the information needed to answer a question is in *one place* within the text. With Think & Search QARs, the reader must search across *multiple places* to construct a complete answer. As readers mature, the definition of *place* will change. In the primary grades, *same place* refers to a single sentence. In the intermediate grades, students generally consider *same place* to be within a single paragraph. By middle school and beyond, readers generally consider *same place* to encompass a larger amount of text—sections, chapters, or when using text sets, an entire book.

Place, in the language of QAR, must remain fluid. For example, students in one fourth-grade classroom noted that a question didn't seem like a Think & Search QAR when they were simply looking at different sentences in the same paragraph. Their teacher agreed, and collaboratively, they decided that they would define *same place* as within a single paragraph. In other cases, the teacher, rather than the students, raised the possibility of expanding the definition of place. We have found that it rarely matters who brings it up, as long as students are ready to reconsider how place is defined to distinguish between Right There and Think & Search QARs.

The Third Paired Comparison: Author & Me/On My Own

The third paired comparison expands In My Head QARs into two categories: Author & Me and On My Own. Both QARs involve questions that require readers to respond using information from their own background knowledge and life experiences. The distinction between the two comes down to the amount of significant, actionable information the reader uses from the text to determine the appropriate background knowledge to access.

On My Own QARs require little or no information from the text for readers to construct a complete and appropriate answer. These QARs are designed to build the reader's knowledge prior to reading or to draw on the reader's experience during the reading process. Author and Me QARs create a bridge between the cognitive strategy or strategies students use to construct the author's intended meaning and personal responses they create to make text-to-self and self-to-text connections. While the information used to answer the question comes from the reader's own knowledge base and life experiences, knowing *what* to access and *why* involves understanding the text. Author & Me QARs underscore the connection between the text and reader's world.

Together, the language of QAR provides a way of talking about the relationships among the purposes for reading, the questions readers are asked or ask themselves, the text source(s), and the readers' knowledge base. When used in the context of comprehension strategy instruction, QAR language can make visible the role of particular strategies in responding to different QARs.

QAR and The Reading Cycle

A second fundamental element of the *QAR Comprehension Lessons* books is the emphasis on how the language of QAR can provide a way to talk about the information sources readers use within the reading cycle, as depicted in Figure 2.

FIGURE 2

BEFORE READING: When drawing on background knowledge (other texts by the same author, similar genres or topics, and so on), teachers and students engage in conversation driven by On My Own QARs as they prepare to enter the text world. A reader who has read part of the text, put it aside, and is now returning to it, or a reader using significant information from the text (e.g., table of contents, headings, charts, images) draws on Author & Me QARs, building from previous readings to anticipate or make predictions about ideas and events before entering the text world.

DURING READING: The dominant QARs are Think & Search and Author & Me, with the occasional Right There QAR asked and answered to highlight important ideas and details. As readers move through the text, they use all the resources they can muster to make sense of what they are reading: identifying key information (Right There or Think & Search), making inferences (Author & Me), summarizing (Think & Search), monitoring to check predictions (Author & Me), and so forth. In effect, they are making text-to-self connections that facilitate meaning construction. However, while in the text world, they also step back and reflect on how content is changing their knowledge and perceptions—not only of the text world but also of their own world. As they reflect, they invoke a range of reader responses (Author & Me) that enhance their engagement with the text.

AFTER READING: Upon leaving the text world, readers respond critically to what they have read, using strategies that support Author & Me QARs. For example, they revisit characters' motivations and how plots have played out. Stories may change the way readers think about aspects of their own lives. They engage in critical analysis of the quality of the text, moving beyond whether or not the text was a "good read" ("I liked this because . . ." "This was useful because . . .") to considering the strengths and weaknesses of the narrative, the argument, or information presented.

Understanding the reading cycle and the QARs that are associated with each phase of the cycle helps readers in several ways. It enables readers to connect the stances they assume toward the text before, during, and after reading; recognize the QARs (knowledge sources) they should draw on during each phase of the cycle; and identify the comprehension strategies useful at various times.

Core Comprehension Strategies

The third fundamental element of the *QAR Comprehension Lessons* is the use of QAR language in teaching students about, and modeling routines for, successful comprehension. Lessons model tools that support cognitive engagement in each of the six comprehension strategies defined in Table 2. The QAR language and lessons enrich students' understanding of what it means to be an active, strategic reader.

Predicting

Predicting, an Author & Me QAR, requires readers to use what they know, shaped by information provided by the text. Before reading, the text information may simply be the title or genre or name of the author that readers use to construct their image of the text world that they are about to enter. During reading, the author provides clues that readers use to consider what will happen next. Ideas for the prediction must, by definition, come from the readers' head (i.e., Me), though the text (i.e., Author) provides important clues about what might be relevant.

Drawing Inferences

Like predicting, drawing inferences is an Author & Me QAR, requiring readers to use text information to guide them as they seek relevant ideas and information from their heads. Readers draw inferences "to arrive at a decision or opinion by reasoning from known facts or evidence" (Fountas & Pinnell, 2001, p. 317). Their decision or opinion comes from their heads, but it is constrained by clues from the author.

Identifying Important Information

Identifying important information requires routines that can be used to answer Think & Search and Right There QARs as readers separate essential from nonessential text content. The important information is In the Book, requiring that readers either Think & Search the text, or if the important information is a single detail, find it Right There in one place.

Summarizing

Summarizing, primarily a Think & Search QAR, builds on the foundation established by identifying important information. Readers reorganize the important information to construct a brief, coherent version of the completed text. Summarizing may reflect Author & Me QAR routines when readers bring their own opinions, warranted by the text, into the condensed version.

Questioning

QARs related to questioning depend on who asks the question. When readers answer questions posed by others (e.g., peers, their teacher, textbooks), they use routines appropriate to the likely QAR. When readers generate questions, Author & Me QARs are most relevant since readers must stay consistent with the text content (Author) while they go beyond the text (Me) to create the question. They cannot generate text-based questions unless they have already read the text, and they have little reason to generate On My Own QARs as these play a lesser role in comprehension instruction during and after reading.

Comprehension Monitoring

Monitoring, like questioning, is primarily Author & Me since readers are engaged in an ongoing process of inquiry about the text. Capable, active readers—when monitoring—are checking their success in accurately predicting, drawing inferences, asking questions, figuring out the important information, and creating accurate summaries. They respond to breakdowns in comprehension by using their own knowledge, guided and shaped by the information the author has provided.

Strategies in Combination

Active readers neither choose a text based on using a given strategy (e.g., so they can summarize or predict), nor use strategies one at a time. They invoke comprehension strategies based on need, usually finding some more useful than others, depending on the phase in the reading cycle (e.g., predicting before reading, summarizing after reading). When students know which strategies are useful for particular QARs, and which QARs are likely to arise at different parts of the reading cycle, they are in a position to understand how to be active and strategic, invoking strategies appropriate to the reading process that can improve their understanding of text.

A Multiyear Approach

The fourth element in *QAR Comprehension Lessons* reflects the importance of a coherent multiyear approach. One year of comprehension instruction is rarely sufficient, even when provided by a highly skilled and experienced teacher who has implemented the shared language of QAR. Further, texts increase in complexity from primary grades to middle school, and students benefit from practice extending their knowledge of strategies to new and more complex situations while learning new tools to support their comprehension of more challenging texts. In our experience, the importance of a multiyear approach holds across all schools. However, it is especially salient in schools serving a high proportion of students who struggle with reading and writing. These students definitely require two, three, or more years of coherent instruction in comprehension instruction—the more, the better.

Coherence is at the heart of what Kathy Au (Au & Raphael, 2011) describes as a *staircase curriculum*. The staircase curriculum is one in which teachers hold a clear vision of the excellent graduating reader and writer—the top step. At each grade level, teachers have a clear understanding of the goals their students must achieve to climb the staircase and achieve this vision. Each stair is steep enough to ensure progress, and there are no cracks in the staircase through which a student might fall.

QAR Comprehension Lessons embodies the concept of the staircase curriculum. Within and across books, the goal is to help students and their teachers develop and use a shared language for talking about comprehension strategy use throughout the reading cycle. Thus, initial lessons focus on introducing the QAR language. Then the QAR language is connected to the reading cycle. Next, lessons focus on the link between strategy use and traversing the reading cycle successfully. Fourth, lessons teach students the formal metacognitive strategy of monitoring this process to support understanding.

Across the books, steps "rise" in terms of text difficulty, routines taught, and balance between oral and written activity. For example, comprehension strategies that involve only a few parts (e.g., predicting) are taught in similar ways across the books, with the staircase reflected in text difficulty and the range of tools introduced to students. With strategies involving multiple parts (e.g., summarizing, monitoring), the lessons differ across the books. Lessons for younger students reflect more collaborative oral work and focus on basic routines or tools readers use. Lessons in the upper grades provide an expanded repertoire of tools and promote increasing independence in applying the tools to more complex texts.

Organization of the QAR Comprehension Lessons Books

The three books in the *QAR Comprehension Lessons* series are designed for use at primary grades (2–3), intermediate grades (4–5), and middle school (6–8). Each book is organized into four sections:

SECTION 1: Lessons 1–3 introduce students to the basic concepts and vocabulary of QAR.

SECTION 2: Lesson 4 connects QAR language to the before, during, and after stages of the reading cycle.

SECTION 3: Lessons 5–14 focus on the five core comprehension strategies. These lessons use QAR language to teach students basic routines and tools for predicting, drawing inferences, identifying important information, summarizing, and questioning in informational and narrative texts.

SECTION 4: Lessons 15 and 16 focus on comprehension monitoring. These lessons help students understand how active readers use the strategies, routines, and tools discussed in Lessons 1–14 to monitor their understanding and invoke relevant solutions in response to comprehension problems in informational and narrative text.

Each lesson moves through the six steps of the gradual release of responsibility instructional model (Pearson, 1985): explicit explanation, modeling, guided practice, coaching, independent application, and self-assessment and goal setting. A lesson can be taught in one extended session but is designed to be taught easily over two days: Day 1 from Explicit Explanation through Guided Practice and Day 2 from Coaching to Self-Assessment & Goal-Setting. An informational or narrative passage accompanies each lesson and is annotated to show which section to use with each step. Sample think-alouds in each lesson show how you might introduce the appropriate QAR and demonstrate its application with the passage as you move from explicit explanation to promoting students' independent application. On the accompanying CD, you'll find whole-class posters and charts to use during instruction and for students' reference during and beyond the lesson; charts and graphics for students to use in small groups, pairs, and individually (or as models to copy onto their own notebook paper); and the passages to copy for student use. These passages provide a balance between informational texts with science, social studies, and mathematics content, and narrative text and poetry, including stories and biographies.

Concluding Comments

We hope that these lessons show that comprehension and comprehension instruction need not be elusive. We have designed them to help teachers navigate the complexities of comprehension instruction. At one level, the lessons are models of how instruction can be scaffolded to move students toward independent application of what they have been taught. At another level, the lessons are models for comprehension instruction of core strategies that research has demonstrated to be central to meaning-making. At yet another level, the lessons provide a window into different grouping arrangements to support student-to-student discussion in pairs and small groups. At their core, the lessons demonstrate how QAR, as a language of instruction, can lead students to take control of their reading processes and gain a deeper understanding of text.

References

Au, K. H., & Raphael, T. E. (2010). Using workshop approaches to support the literacy development of English language learners. In G. Li, & P. A. Edwards (Eds.). *Best practices in ELL instruction* (pp. 207–221). New York: Guilford.

Au, K. H., & Raphael, T. E. (2011). Building a staircase curriculum. *New England Journal of Reading, 46*(2), 1–8.

Dole, J. A., Duffy, G. G., Roehler, L. R., & Pearson, P. D. (1991). Moving from the old to the new: Research on reading comprehension instruction. *Review of Educational Research, 61*(2), 239–264.

Fountas, I., & Pinnell, G. S. (2001). *Guiding readers and writers, Grades 3–6: Teaching comprehension, genre, and content literacy.* Westport, CT: Heinemann.

Harvey, S., & Goudvis, A. (2007). *Strategies that work.* Portland, MA: Stenhouse.

Hoyt, L. (2005). *Spotlight on comprehension: Building a literacy of thoughtfulness.* Westport, CT: Heinemann.

Israel, S. E. D., & Duffy, G. G.(Eds.). (2009). *Handbook of research on reading comprehension.* New York: Taylor & Francis.

McLaughlin, M., & Allen, M. B. (2009). *Guided comprehension in Grades 3–8* (2nd Ed.). Newark, DE: International Reading Association.

Pearson, P. D. (1985). Changing the face of reading comprehension instruction. *The Reading Teacher, 38*(6), 724–738.

Raphael, T. E., & Au, K. H. (in press). In J. Paratore & R.L. McCormack (Eds.), *After early intervention: Then what?* (2nd Ed.). Newark, DE: International Reading Association.

Raphael, T. E., Highfield, K., & Au, K. H. (2006). *QAR now: A powerful and practical framework that develops comprehension and higher-level thinking in all students.* New York: Scholastic.

Raphael, T. E., George, M.A., Weber, C. M., & Nies, A. (2009). Approaches to teaching reading comprehension. In S. E. Israel & G. G. Duffy (Eds.). *Handbook of research on reading comprehension* (pp. 449–469). New York: Taylor and Francis.

In the Book/In My Head QARs

GOAL • Introducing QAR language: In the Book and In My Head

I Can Statement

I know the difference between In the Book and In My Head QARs and can use this knowledge to improve my comprehension.

Materials *(See CD for Reproducibles.)*

▶ "Is Txting 2 Much Bad 4 U?" by Karen Fanning (Informational passage), p. 20 (display copy, one copy for each student)

▶ QAR Information Sources Poster (display copy)

▶ QAR Self-Assessment Thinksheet (one copy for each student)

BEFORE READING DURING READING AFTER READING

Step **1** EXPLICIT EXPLANATION

Tell students that today you will teach them how to identify two main sources of information for creating good answers for questions about what they read. Display the I Can Statement and refer to key terms (QAR, In the Book, In My Head) as you read it aloud to introduce the lesson.

> *We are learning about QARs today. QAR stands for Question Answer Relationships. When I am trying to gain a good understanding of what I'm reading, I find it helpful to think of two different sources of information. One main source of information is In the Book. An In the Book QAR involves any written text—not just books—including magazines, newspapers, online documents or other digital sources, and images. The second main source I use is In My Head. This QAR refers to my own background knowledge and experiences.*

Display the QAR Information Sources Poster.

> *What you learn today about QAR will help you comprehend what you are reading in or out of school, on tests, and online. Good readers often ask themselves questions as they read to check their understanding and remember important ideas. Sometimes, others ask us questions—friends interested in knowing more about a text, teachers checking our understanding, and questions printed in reading materials. QAR helps us use the information available to us from the source (the text—In the Book) and from our own knowledge base (In My Head) in strategic ways to improve our learning and our question-answering.*

Step 2 MODELING

Display and read aloud the title of the passage, "Is Txting 2 Much Bad 4 U?"

> *The question in the title gives me clues to think about what I know about texting and my experiences with it. The title also starts me thinking about what the passage will be about. I start using information In My Head when I think about how I would answer this question even before I begin reading. But I also suspect that information In the Book might teach me something different from what I had thought or might give me new information. In the Book information can also provide facts to support what I had In My Head.*

Post the following questions, then display and read aloud the first two paragraphs of the passage.

1. Why do teenagers text a lot? [*In My Head: possible answer: access to cell phones, can "talk" to many friends*]

2. What are some negative consequences of excessive texting? [*In the Book: distracts from schoolwork, interrupts sleep, causes thumb injuries from repetitive motion*]

> *Now that I have read the first part of the text, I am going to use the two information sources, In the Book and In My Head, as I answer these questions. First, I think about which of the two sources is most likely to help me with each question. Even when I have an answer In My Head, I should check In the Book for anything new I can learn. To answer the first question, I need to provide reasons why teenagers text a lot. The author did not provide any information to answer this question, so I know this is an In My Head QAR. I have to draw on my own background knowledge and experiences to answer this question using information In My Head.*

Provide a few reasons, such as the ones shown beside the question and/or elicit ideas from students.

> *The second question is an In the Book QAR. In the passage, I see the words "excessive texting" and "host of problems," and I know that I can use the information in the rest of that sentence to answer this question.*

Share one reason and then ask students to complete the answer to the second question.

Step 3 GUIDED PRACTICE

Distribute a copy of the passage to each student. Display the next two questions.

> *Let's read the next two paragraphs of the passage and work together to identify the information source for the following two questions:*

1. What are the signs that Kate Morrissey is texting excessively? [*In the Book: sends and receives as many as 60 texts a day at home, in the car, at brother's games, at movies, in restaurants; less than average but 20 more than sent in 2007*]

2. How are your texting habits similar to or different from Kate Morrissey's? [*In My Head: Answers will vary depending on students' experiences.*]

Read aloud the next section or ask volunteers to read as the other students follow along. Guide students to use what they have learned about the two QARs to identify the information source and relevant information for answering the questions.

Step 4 COACHING

Then have partners read the next section "It's Really Addicting."

> *Use what you learned about In the Book and In My Head QARs as you work with a partner to read "It's Really Addicting" and answer questions about that section. For each question, first determine the best information source—In the Book or In My Head—and then answer the question. Be prepared to justify your choice of information source and the quality of your answer information using that source.*

While students work, monitor and facilitate their use of the two core QARs. Provide additional support as needed. When some students begin to finish the reading, display the following questions:

1. What are some effects of texting during class? [*In the Book: distracting, not paying attention, not learning, poor grades*]

2. Describe two ways that texting affects Molly Reape's life. [*In the Book: lack of sleep, annoyed with friends, addicted—reluctant to turn off phone even when bothered by it*]

3. How does texting affect your life? [*In My Head: Answers will vary.*]

When students have completed the task, ask two pairs to form a square (4 students) and compare their QAR selections and answers. Call on two or three squares to explain their answers and describe the information source they used.

Step 5 INDEPENDENT APPLICATION

> *You are getting good at using QAR knowledge to improve your comprehension. Now I want you to use QAR on your own.*

Display the final two questions shown below.

> *Read the entire text, including the final section, "Staying Connected." When you have finished reading, answer the two questions displayed. Indicate the QAR—In the Book or In My Head—you will use to answer the question, and then write your answer. Be prepared to share your evidence.*

1. What are some of the benefits of texting? [*In the Book: allows teens to form social bonds with ease, achieves intimacy, enables easy social planning*]

2. Do you think "txting 2 much" is "bad 4 U?" [*In My Head: Answers may vary, but students should use the text to support their conclusion.*]

Step **6** SELF-ASSESSMENT & GOAL SETTING

Allow several students to share their answers and evidence. Then return their focus to the goal of the lesson in preparation for completing their QAR Self-Assessment Thinksheet. Display and revisit the I Can Statement. Remind students that understanding QARs can support their understanding of text and response to questions.

> *Now I would like you to think about how you can use this strategy in other areas and how you can add this to your own personal toolkit for reading.*

Have students complete a QAR Self-Assessment Thinksheet and turn it in along with the answers to the five questions from the Coaching and Independent Application steps.

Is Txting 2 Much Bad 4 U?

By Karen Fanning

For use with Step 2: Modeling: title and first 2 paragraphs

When it comes to teens and texting, many people are asking, "How much is too much?" A recent study by the Nielsen Company found that U.S. kids ages 13 to 17 sent and received an average of 2,272 texts per month in the last quarter of 2008. That's about 80 messages a day—more than double the average of 2007!

Is this cause for alarm? Doctors and psychologists warn that excessive texting may be leading to a host of problems, including distractions from schoolwork, interrupted sleep, and thumb injuries caused by too much repetitive motion.

For use with Step 3: Guided Practice: next 2 paragraphs

How can you tell if you're at risk? "It's too much when it starts to interfere with the other activities in your life, like school, homework, or sports," Michael Hausauer, an adolescent psychotherapist in Oakland, California, tells *Junior Scholastic*. "When you can't put [your keypad] away and return to it later, then it's become too big a part of your life."

There are days, says Kate Morrissey, 14, when she sends and receives as many as 60 text messages. "I text at home, in the car when I'm going somewhere, at my brother's games, at the movies before it starts, in restaurants," the ninth-grader from Hingham, Massachusetts, tells *Junior Scholastic*.

It's Really Addicting

For use with Step 4: Coaching: "It's Really Addicting" section

Molly Reape, 12, also finds plenty of time to text, despite a busy schedule that includes dance class five days a week. "If I have a second anywhere, I'll text," says the seventh-grader from Scituate, Massachusetts. "It's really addicting."

On average, Molly exchanges a few dozen messages a day with friends. At night, she keeps her cell phone beside her bed. Sometimes, she is interrupted by friends texting her as she drifts off to sleep.

"When someone starts texting me when I'm falling asleep, I'll say, 'I'm really tired now, I'm going to bed,'" she says. "If I don't respond to them, they'll keep texting me, 'Are you there, are you there?' It gets really annoying."

Still, Molly is reluctant to turn off her phone. "Just in case someone has to tell me something really important," she says, "I keep it on."

That, says Hausauer, is not wise. "Young people need to be able to say good night to their technology," he tells *Junior Scholastic*.

What about saying goodbye to their technology at the classroom door? Texting during class is also on the rise. Because kids can exchange messages silently, they often do so without getting caught.

Students who text in class, says Diego Fernandez-Pages, 12, may end up paying a price at test time. "Texting is really distracting," says the eighth-grader from Brookline, Massachusetts. "You definitely aren't paying attention if you're texting. [Therefore], you won't be learning anything. . . . When you are quizzed or tested, you probably would not get a good grade."

Staying Connected

For use with Step 5: Independent Application: "Staying Connected" section

Still, texting does allow teens to form social bonds with ease. "The need for intimacy at that age is so powerful," says Carolyn Meyer-Wartels, a social worker in New York City. "[Texting] is a way for kids to stay connected in a hectic, over-programmed world."

Kate agrees. Because of texting, she can easily keep in touch with her cousins in Virginia and with friends whom she sees only during the summer.

As for her hometown pals, Kate says that texting has made her social life much easier to manage. "I hang out with a big group of friends," Kate tells *Junior Scholastic*. "I have to check with a lot of people to make plans. I can just send them a quick text, rather than calling them back every five minutes."

To determine whether your texting habits are healthy, you need to answer one simple question: "Am I in charge of texting, or is texting in charge of me?" says Hausauer. "I'm in charge when I decide when I'm going to text and when I'm going to stop. If you feel overly worried or anxious when you turn your phone off, you may have a problem."

Right There/Think & Search QARs

GOAL • Introduce the two types of In the Book QARs: Right There and Think & Search

I Can Statement

I can distinguish between Right There and Think & Search QARs and use this knowledge to improve my comprehension.

Materials *(See CD for reproducibles.)*

▶ "Would You Drink Toilet Water?" by Emily Costello (informational passage), p. 24 (display copy, one copy for each student)

▶ In the Book QARs Poster (display copy)

▶ QAR Self-Assessment Thinksheet (one copy for each student)

| BEFORE READING | DURING READING | AFTER READING |

Step **1** EXPLICIT EXPLANATION

Ask students to recall the two types of QARs introduced in Lesson 1: In the Book and In My Head. Display the I Can Statement and ask students to read it. Then tell students that in this lesson they will learn to distinguish between the two types of In the Book QARs:

▶ Right There

▶ Think & Search

Display the In the Book QARs Poster and introduce the concept:

> *The key difference between Right There and Think & Search QARs is the location of the information you need for a complete answer to a question. The information for either one will be located in the text. Sometimes, the information is Right There in one place; for example, the two sentences that contain the answer are right next to one another. Other times, the information you need is spread out across the text, so you have to Think & Search in several different places to find it; for example, you might have to look across paragraphs, in a chart and a paragraph, or across sections or chapters.*

> *We'll be using the passage "Would You Drink Toilet Water?" to practice using these In the Book QARs.*

Step 2 MODELING

Display the passage and the two questions shown below. Indicate that you will keep these questions in mind as you read, since you know them in advance.

1. What location provides its customers with tap water that comes partly from sewage? [*Right There: Orange County, California*]

2. What happened to the fresh water there that led to the use of treated sewage in the tap water system? [*Think & Search: less precipitation than normal, led to a drought, water sources dried up; must import water*]

Read the title and first two paragraphs aloud.

> *My first step is to decide which QAR can help me identify the information I'll need for my answer. I recognize that all the information I need to answer both these questions is In the Book. Some are Right There in one place, but other answers will require me to Think & Search across the text. Since the words "tap water" and the words "residents," and "northern and central Orange County, California" can be found in one place, it means that Question 1 is a Right There QAR. (Point to the words in the passage as you think aloud.) To answer Question 2, I need to Think & Search across several places in the text to find everything I need to answer the question completely. (As you think aloud, highlight or underline the information in the text; see the answer shown above.) I had to use the information from several sentences across the two paragraphs.*

Step 3 GUIDED PRACTICE

Hand out a copy of the passage to each student. Display the following questions:

1. Why did Orange County officials consider toilet water as a potential source for tap water? [*Right There: guaranteed supply of water*]

2. What is the purification process for the toilet water? [*Think & Search: capture the flushed wastewater, run it through standard sewage treatment, then send it through purification process*]

3. How many steps does the purification process have? [*Answers may vary: Right There: "three-step purification process" or Think & Search: "three-step," "traps contaminants"; "removes salt, drugs, chemicals, viruses"; "kills living contaminants that remain"*]

> *Listen as I read the next two paragraphs. Then I will ask you to use what you know about Right There and Think & Search QARs so that we can answer these questions.*

Guide students to identify the QARs and answer the questions. Note that the third question can be either Right There or Think & Search depending on the information that students choose to use. Either answer is acceptable as long students can justify their reasoning. You might point out that the Right There answer is less complete than the Think & Search answer and then discuss which one could be considered the better answer.

Step 4 COACHING

Display the following questions:

1. What happens to the treated sewage water? [*Think & Search: Half is injected into the ground near the coast to stop saltwater from flowing into the groundwater basin. The other half is pumped into lakes where it eventually ends up in the groundwater basin.*]

2. What is a groundwater basin? [*Right There: a rocky area beneath the ground where fresh water collects.*]

Now I want you to practice with a partner. Read the next two paragraphs of the passage. Then use your understanding of Right There and Think & Search QARs to help you answer these two questions. First, identify the QAR, then write your answer to the question, and be prepared to share the text evidence you used to answer each question.

While students work, provide additional support as needed (e.g., underlining Think & Search information to use to answer questions, scanning for Right There information). Ask two or three pairs to share their QARs, corresponding answers, and reasons for choosing each QAR.

Step 5 INDEPENDENT APPLICATION

Display the final two questions:

1. How have Orange County residents reacted to drinking the purified tap water? [*Think & Search: Some would drink it (Vincent, Liz), but others find it too gross (Becky, others in the public who agree with her).*]

2. How did the water treatment officials address the claim that the water was too clean to drink? [*Right There: added back salts and minerals to make it taste more natural*]

Now I want you to try it on your own. Please read the last section, "Drink Up," on your own. Then identify whether the QAR is Right There or Think & Search and answer the questions. Be prepared to share the evidence you used.

Step 6 SELF-ASSESSMENT AND GOAL SETTING

Ask partners to share their responses to these questions: *What is one thing you learned about In the Book QARs today that could help improve your text comprehension and your ability to answer questions? Where is one place—in or out of school—where you could use this knowledge?*

Have a few pairs to share their ideas. Then revisit the I Can Statement. Ask students to think about their responses to the questions statement and how they can add this strategy to their own personal toolkit for reading. Finally, have them complete the QAR Self-Assessment Thinksheet and turn it in with their answers to the final two questions.

Would You Drink Toilet Water?

By Emily Costello

For use with Step 2: Modeling: title and first 2 paragraphs

When residents in northern and central Orange County, California, turn on the tap, some of the water that fills their glass comes from an unlikely source—sewage. The water has been cleaned, but would you want to drink it?

Driven by Drought

From 2000 to 2007, the western United States experienced lower than usual precipitation, which led to severe drought conditions. That was bad news for Orange County, which imports roughly 50 percent of its water supply. Some of that water comes from as far away as the Colorado River. The prolonged drought caused supplies of the imported water to dry up.

For use with Step 3: Guided Practice: next 2 paragraphs

To keep up with the county's water demands, officials had to think outside the box. They soon turned their attention to an unlikely source: toilet water. "It's a guaranteed supply of water," says Shivaji Deshmukh, the program manager for the Orange County Groundwater Replenishment System—the system responsible for making the water from restroom potties suitable for use in kitchen pots.

The Journey

How does the county's water go from toilet to tap? Here's what happens: The sewage department captures wastewater flushed in toilets in northern and central Orange County near Los Angeles. It runs the water through a standard sewage treatment plant, where it comes out clean enough to be dumped into the ocean. But rather than head seaward, the water flows through an elaborate system of pipes, filters, and tanks, where it undergoes a three-step purification process. The purification process traps large contaminants like bacteria; removes salt, prescription drugs, chemicals, and viruses; and kills any living contaminants that may still be present.

For use with Step 4: Coaching: next 2 paragraphs

After the steps are completed, half of the treated water is injected into the ground near the coast. That water stops salty Pacific Ocean water from flowing into the groundwater basin, a rocky area beneath the ground where fresh water collects. The other half is pumped into lakes, where it seeps down slowly through layers of clay and rock and eventually ends up in the groundwater basin too.

Months later, when Orange County residents turn on their tap, that water will help quench their thirst. It will even help fill bottles at a bottled water company there!

Drink Up

For use with Step 5: Independent Application: "Drink Up" section

Not everyone loves the idea of downing water that once swished through toilet pipes. "I wouldn't want to drink it just because I knew it had been in gross places," says Becky Edwards, age 14, from Connecticut.

Becky is not alone. Construction of plants like the one in Orange County has been blocked in other California places like San Diego because of public disgust with the idea of drinking water that once contained—well, poop.

But does the treated water taste yucky? Not at all, Deshmukh insists. He claims the water is actually *too* clean to drink, thanks to the three-step purification process. At the end, officials have to add back a few salts and minerals to make it more like natural water.

"Some people may think it's nasty to drink the water in Orange County," says Liz Garrido, a 15-year-old from Santa Ana. "But to me, the water is pretty clean, because it is purified before we drink it."

Vincent DePinto, another California teen, agrees. He visited the water treatment plant in August. At the end of the tour, a guide gave each visitor a glass of newly treated water to drink. "At first I felt a little freaked out," admits Vincent. "But it tasted very good, just like normal water."

Author & Me/On My Own QARs

GOAL • Introduce the two types of In My Head Book QARs: Author & Me and On My Own

I Can Statement

I can distinguish between Author & Me and On My Own QARs and use this knowledge to improve my comprehension.

Materials *(See CD for reproducibles.)*

▶ "Around the World at 17" (narrative passage), p. 29 (display copy, one copy for each student)

▶ In My Head QARs Poster (display copy)

▶ QAR Self-Assessment Thinksheet (one copy for each student)

BEFORE READING   DURING READING   AFTER READING

Step **1** EXPLICIT EXPLANATION

Remind students of the two types of QARs introduced in Lesson 1—In the Book and In My Head—and that they have already learned about the two kinds of In the Book QARs: Right There and Think & Search.

Display the In My Head QARs Poster. Tell students that in this lesson they will learn about the two kinds of In My Head QARs: Author & Me and On My Own.

> *Sometimes, when I use an In My Head QAR to an answer a question, I have to use the clues from the author to know which background knowledge to use. This type of QAR is called Author & Me. I can answer other questions without any clues from the author or the text. I can even answer these questions without reading the passage. This type of QAR is called On My Own.*

Step **2** MODELING

Display the passage. Read aloud the title and the first five paragraphs, pausing to think aloud as you share your thoughts about the text with students. Then display the following questions:

> 1. What is something adventurous that you have done? [*On My Own: Answers will vary, depending on students' experiences.*]

2. Would you want to have an adventure like Zac's? Explain why or why not. [*Author & Me: Answers will vary but should cite evidence from the text about Zac's adventure.*]

Now that I have read the beginning of the text, I'm going to identify the QARs to help me answer these two questions. The first question asks about one of my own adventures. I don't need to compare it to Zac's adventure, so I can answer this one On My Own without any clues from the author. (Model by briefly describing an adventure you have had.) The second question asks if I would want to have an adventure like Zac's. This answer must come from my head, but I also need to think about Zac's adventure before I can answer it. Would I want to have an adventure where I was alone in dangerous situations? Would I want to have an adventure that involved sailing? I couldn't answer this question without reading and understanding the text, even though the answer must come from In My Head, too. So this In My Head QAR is an Author & Me.

Step 3 GUIDED PRACTICE

Distribute a copy of the passage to each student.

Now I want you to practice using In My Head QARs. Follow along as I read the section called "Boating Background." Then I will ask you to use what you know about the two In My Head QARs—Author & Me and On My Own—to answer two more questions.

After you read the section, display the following questions:

1. Based on what you've learned so far about Zac, how well do you think he is prepared for this trip? Provide reasons for your answer. [*Author & Me: Yes: extensive boating experience, seemingly responsible about earning money for a boat, able to repair the boat if he needed to since he and his dad got it ready. No, he is young, had never sailed alone before.*]

2. How would you prepare for a sailing trip around the world? [*On My Own: Answers will vary based on students' knowledge of and experiences with sailing.*]

For the first question, guide students to identify clues in the text that describe Zac's background. Emphasize that they had to read the text to know how Zac prepared for the trip, but determining whether this was good or not was based on their own judgment and reasoning. Contrast this with the second question, which is related to the text but could be answered even if students had not read or understood it.

Step 4 COACHING

Have partners read the next section "Adventures at Sea" and answer questions about this part of the text.

> *Now that you have practiced using Author & Me and On My Own QARs with me to improve comprehension, I want you to work with a partner to read the next section of text and answer two questions that relate to it. Decide together which QAR you think is the most appropriate to use to answer each question and to create your best answer for it.*

Display the following questions as students begin to read together:

1. Which of Zac's experiences do you think were the most harrowing? Why? [*Author & Me: Answers will vary but should describe Zac's specific experiences and justify why it (or they) would be worse than the others. This question also requires readers to know what "harrowing" means.*]

2. What would you bring for entertainment if you were going to be by yourself for several months? [*On My Own: Answers will vary based on students' interests.*]

While students work, monitor and facilitate their use of Author & Me and On My Own QARs. Ask two pairs to form a square (4 students) and compare their QAR choices and answers. Then have several pairs share their responses with the whole class. Point out that thinking about the QAR—whether Author & Me or On My Own—helps readers know the sources of information they should use to answer a question.

Step 5 INDEPENDENT APPLICATION

Ask students to read the last section "Big World to Explore" on their own.

> *Now that you have practiced identifying In My Head QARs with a partner, I want you to try it on your own. Please read the final section of the passage. Then identify the QAR—either Author & Me or On My Own—and answer the questions I show you. For each question, identify the QAR, answer it, and be prepared to share the information you used.*

While students are reading, display the following questions:

1. What do you think Zac learned by sailing alone around the world? [*Author & Me: Answers will vary but should mention events from the trip that would have pushed Zac's abilities, his ability to think in new ways. The emphasis here is on using text to justify their thinking.*]

2. In what ways do you think teenagers are capable of accomplishing more than society assumes? [*On My Own: Answers will vary depending on students' individual experiences. QAR could be Author & Me if students justify their response to Zac's experiences as their sole justification rather than using their own experiences and views.*]

Allow students time to complete the reading, identify the QARs, answer the questions, and prepare to share their answers and evidence. Call on a few students to share their work.

Step 6 SELF-ASSESSMENT AND GOAL SETTING

To wrap up the lesson, ask the following question: *How did knowing about Author & Me and On My Own—the two In My Head QARs—help you answer the questions about this passage?*

Ask several students to share their ideas. To prepare them for completing the QAR Self-Assessment Thinksheet, read aloud the I Can Statement to return their focus to the goal of the lesson:

> *I can distinguish between Author & Me and On My Own QARs and use this knowledge to improve my comprehension.*

Ask students to indicate whether they agree or disagree with this statement. Have those who agree share ideas of other areas where they can use QAR to help them comprehend what they are reading. Make a note of students who do not agree with this statement— they are likely to need additional explanation and practice with distinguishing the two In My Head QARs. Distribute a copy of the QAR Self-Assessment Thinksheet to each student to complete independently. Collect the thinksheet and their responses to the questions in the Coaching and Independent Application steps.

Around the World at 17

For use with Step 2: Modeling:

title and first 5 paragraphs

On July 16, 2009, Zac Sunderland sailed into Marina del Rey in Los Angeles County, California, on a 36-foot sailboat named *Intrepid* to a soundtrack of air horns, whirring helicopters, and cheering. Why all the fuss? Zac had just become the first person to complete a solo trip around the world before the age of 18.

Zac began his 28,000-mile journey 13 months earlier, on June 14, 2008. He made the decision to go only six months before that.

"Football season was over," Zac jokes, "and I was looking for something to do."

A solo circumnavigation might not be what most people would expect a high-school student to choose, but Zac isn't interested in doing what people expect. He thinks teens are capable of much more than society assumes.

"I wanted to experience life," says Zac.

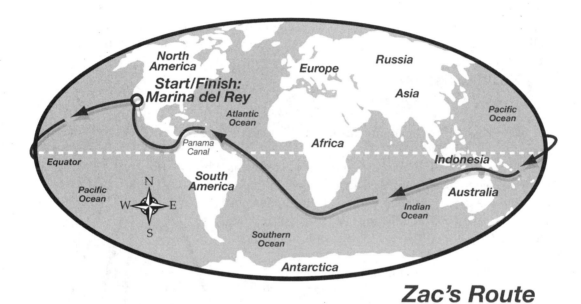

Zac's Route

For use with Step 3: Guided Practice:

"Boating Background" section

Boating Background

Zac's trip was inspired in part by Robin Lee Graham's book, *Dove*. In *Dove*, Graham describes his own five-year trip sailing around the world. He started his journey in 1965 at the age of 16.

Zac's introduction to the world of sailing came before he read Graham's book, however. "I learned how to sail before I could ride a bike," says Zac. His dad is a shipwright (a person who builds and repairs boats), and both of his parents are experienced sailors. But although Zac had done a lot of sailing with his family, his first solo trip would be the one he took around the world.

Zac used the $6,000 he'd saved from summer jobs to buy a sailboat. He and his dad then spent four months getting it ready.

When they were finished, Zac knew *Intrepid* was up to the trip. The only question was how he would hold up.

For use
with Step 4:
Coaching:
"Adventures at
Sea" section

Adventures at Sea

Zac made it safely around the planet—but not without some harrowing moments. One of the most perilous situations occurred on the Indian Ocean. The wind ripped loose the heavy wire that helps support the mast (the tall pole that holds the sails), and the mast was in danger of breaking. For two days and nights, as wild waves tossed the boat and the wind whipped at the sails, Zac struggled to make repairs.

Another time, Zac was working on deck around 2 a.m. when *Intrepid* was struck by a "rogue" wave—an unpredictable, abnormally large wave that seems to come from nowhere. While Zac clung to the mast to avoid being swept overboard, the wave soaked the cabin and shorted out the boat's electrical system.

And then there were the pirates. Off the coast of Indonesia, Zac was followed by what he believes was a pirate vessel. He emerged from the ordeal unharmed, but the hour during which it occurred seemed to be the longest hour of Zac's life.

Not all of Zac's days were so dramatic. A friend gave him 70 books to take on the trip, and Zac made his way through almost all of them. He also had an iPod and a collection of DVDs to enjoy in calmer moments. He even spent time updating the blog he kept during the journey.

Big World to Explore

For use
with Step 5:
Independent
Application:

"Big World
to Explore"
section'

For Zac, the best thing about his trip was meeting new people. "I've got friends all over the world," he says proudly. For example, he made many friends during his time in Cape Town, South Africa.

He also loved visiting islands that are accessible only by boat and seeing beautiful places that he wouldn't otherwise see. One island he particularly loved is Saint Helena in the South Atlantic Ocean. Of the island with only 3,000 citizens, Zac says, "There are more people at my high school."

Now Zac is ready to find his next adventure. "I don't like sitting still," he says. He signed with a talent agency, and there is talk of his next adventure—whatever it may be—being made into a TV show.

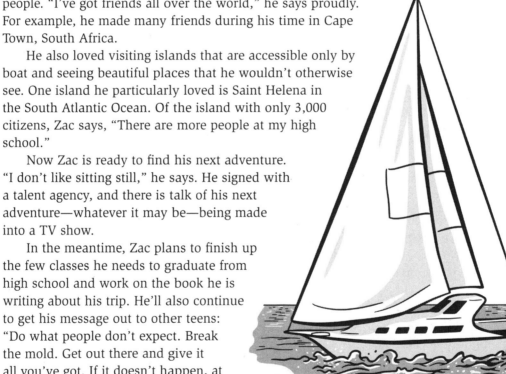

In the meantime, Zac plans to finish up the few classes he needs to graduate from high school and work on the book he is writing about his trip. He'll also continue to get his message out to other teens: "Do what people don't expect. Break the mold. Get out there and give it all you've got. If it doesn't happen, at least you know you tried."

QAR and the Reading Cycle

GOAL • Teach students about QARs and the reading cycle

I Can Statement

I can use QARs to improve my comprehension throughout the reading cycle: before reading, during reading, and after reading.

Materials *(See CD for reproducibles.)*

▶ "Star Trek Tech" by Karina Hamalainen (informational passage), p.37 (display copy, one copy for each student)

▶ I Can Statement written on chart or sentence strip

▶ The Core QARs Poster (display copy)

▶ QAR and the Reading Cycle Poster (display copy)

▶ QAR Self-Assessment Thinksheet (one copy for each student)

Step **1** EXPLICIT EXPLANATION

Today's lesson focuses on the reading cycle (before, during, and after reading) and is designed to help students know how to apply QARs during each part of this cycle. Display the I Can Statement and the QAR and the Reading Cycle Poster.

> *Today we are going to learn about the three parts of the reading cycle—before reading, during reading, and after reading—and how QARs can help you comprehend through each part of this cycle. As a reader, you have already experienced the entire reading cycle, although you may not have called it that. The first part of the reading cycle is called "before reading." This includes what you do before you start reading, such as brainstorming what you already know about the topic, author, or genre. The second part of the reading cycle is called "during reading." This includes what you do while you read a text, such as figuring out the important ideas and connections among those ideas. As you've probably guessed, the third part of the reading cycle is called "after reading." This includes what you do when you've finished reading, such as thinking about the new information you've learned, main ideas or the author's message, and connections between the text and your own lives.*

Next make the connection between the reading cycle and QARs.

> *Certain QARs are more common before, during, or after reading. Knowing which QAR you're likely to encounter in each part of the reading cycle can guide you to make*

the best use of In my Head and In the Book information. As we read the passage "Star Trek Tech," we'll explore which QAR works best with each part of the reading cycle.

Display The Core QARs Poster and briefly review the four different QARs with students.

Step 2 MODELING

BEFORE READING DURING READING AFTER READING

Tell students that active readers use their knowledge of QARs to generate useful questions and to respond to questions posed by others before, during, and after reading. Display the passage and the following questions:

1. What types of futuristic technology are shown in the *Star Trek* series? [*On My Own: Answers will vary but are likely to include technology such as space stations, individual space pods for travel, transporters, holographic entertainment rooms, medical devices, tricorders, and warp drive. Some but not all of these appear in the article.*]

2. What information do you think this article will convey? [*Author & Me: Answers will vary, but possible predictions may include the special effects and props used in TV shows and movies, as well as whether scientists think this technology is possible in the future.*]

Let's start with thinking about the QARs we use most often before reading, which is the first part of the reading cycle. I'll look at the title and the author for clues. I don't recognize the author's name, but I do have some ideas based on the title. The questions you see are ones that I might ask myself, or that I might ask you, before reading.

Have students read the questions aloud with you and discuss the QARs and possible answers. Sample answers appear beside each question above. For the first question, guide students to see the best QAR to use is On My Own because it involves brainstorming before reading based on what readers know from the *Star Trek* television series and movies. For the second question, show that the best QAR to use is Author & Me because it involves prediction, and the answer has to be confirmed by what the author has written.

Conclude this section of the lesson by making sure students understand that On My Own and Author & Me are the types of QARs commonly used *before reading*.

Note: Before reading, we are defining On My Own QARs as those that occur when students are brainstorming based on minimal information about the text—title, opening illustration, author's name, and genre. When we move from brainstorming to predicting before reading, by definition the QAR shifts from On My Own (my opinion about the possibilities) to Author & Me (my predictions have to make sense based on author information).

Step 3 GUIDED PRACTICE

In this step, move to the during-reading part of the reading cycle.

> *We're ready now for the second part of the reading cycle, which is called during reading. During reading, I'm immersing myself in the world of the text. I think about the important ideas, I put these important ideas together, and I monitor my comprehension to make sure everything is making sense.*
>
> *The QARs most valuable to use during reading are Right There, Think & Search, and Author & Me. Right There QARs are useful for helping me identify key ideas in the text that are important for understanding. Think & Search QARs help me make connections among text ideas found in more than one place in the text. Author & Me QARs enable me to draw inferences and monitor my understanding.*

Distribute a copy of the passage to students and display the following questions:

3. Approximately how many atoms are in the human body?

4. What are the major challenges involved in moving people by instantaneous transport?

5. In terms of instantaneous transport, what have researchers been able to accomplish, compared to what the transporter on the *Starship Enterprise* can do?

6. Based on what you have read, do you think a transporter for human beings could be invented? Explain your thinking.

Tell students that these are examples of the kinds of questions active readers might ask themselves during reading.

> *During-reading QARs differ from before-reading QARs. During-reading QARs help readers understand the text by focusing on important ideas in the text, putting those ideas together, and making relevant inferences. None of these during-reading questions is likely to be an On My Own QAR even if I have watched all the Star Trek TV episodes and the movies. I have to look In the Book for information to answer them. Some look like the QAR might be Right There with the answer located in one place, while I might have to Think & Search for others, which will require me to look in several places for the information I need. Still others might be Author & Me QARs, where I will use clues from the text to help me decide what information In My Head will be most useful.*

Have students follow along as you read the "Transporters" section aloud. Then discuss each question in terms of the QAR, the information used to answer the question, and the evidence to support the choice of QAR. Promote the gradual release of responsibility to students in the following manner:

▶ **Question 3:** Read the question, identify the QAR, and use it to model your information search. Ask students to provide evidence to support the choice of QAR and answer [*Right There: Information is stated in one place; 10 octillion*].

▶ **Question 4:** Read the question and identify the QAR. Ask students to search for appropriate information and to provide evidence to confirm the QAR and answer [*Think & Search: Information is found in all three paragraphs about transporters; the major challenges are that it would take the energy of 1,000 hydrogen bombs to dematerialize a person, that it would be extremely complicated to put all of a person's atoms back in the right place, and that researchers have to date only been able to transport individual electrons*].

▶ **Question 5:** Read the question. Ask students to provide the QAR, answer, and evidence to justify the QAR and answer [*Think & Search: Information is contained in the first and third paragraphs about transporters; researchers have been able to instantaneously transport individual electrons, whereas the transporter on the Starship Enterprise can move people from one location to another*]. Students with considerable background knowledge of *Star Trek* and transporters may suggest that the QAR is Author & Me. Accept this answer as long as they can provide a sound justification for their choice of QAR.

▶ **Question 6:** Have students work with a partner. Ask them to read the question and then discuss the QAR, evidence to justify it, and the answer. [*Author & Me: Information is presented in the third paragraph about transporters. Answers to this question will vary. A range of answers is acceptable, provided that students give good reasons for their answers. Example: "I think it may be possible to invent a transporter for humans, because researchers have been able to instantaneously transport individual electrons, and there may be great advances in science in the future."*]

Write down the QAR next to each question. Ask students to describe any patterns they see. Elicit that the types of QARs that occur during reading are primarily Think & Search but may also be Right There or Author & Me. If students do not notice the absence of On My Own QARs, point this out, and note that it is unusual to ask or be asked On My Own questions during reading.

Step 4 COACHING

Tell students that they will be working with a partner to apply what they have learned about QAR and the reading cycle as they read the sections "Sickbay" and "Tricorders" together. Display the following questions:

7. Why does the author say, "Medicine is one area where we are rapidly catching up with *Star Trek*?"

8. What are the advantages of the new portable mass spectrometers compared to older models?

9. Describe a real-life problem on Earth that could be solved if people used a mass spectrometer.

Have each student copy these questions on a sheet of paper, leaving about four lines between the questions so there is adequate space to write the QAR, reasons for choosing it, and the answer to the question. Display the words "QAR," "reason," and "answer" and remind students to include all three for each question. Let students know that it's all right if partners disagree about the QARs and answers, as long as each of them can write down good reasons for the decisions. After partners have discussed the QAR, reason, and answer for each question, each student should write down the information in his or her own words.

Circulate around the room and provide students with guidance as needed. Be sure they know how to use the words in the question to help them locate the text information they need. QARs, reasons, and possible answers for the questions appear below.

▶ **Question 7:** Right There or Think & Search: Students are likely to identify the QAR as Think & Search. However, the QAR depends on whether students decide that the information is in the same place (because it's all contained in one paragraph) or in different places (because it's spread across several sentences). Possible answer: Doctors are now able to use devices much like those in _Star Trek_. They can use noninvasive scanners to take pictures inside the body, lasers to perform surgery, and devices that can give people shots without using a needle.

▶ **Question 8:** Right There or Think & Search. As with the preceding question, Think & Search is the probable choice, but the QAR depends on students' ideas about whether information is in the same place or different places. Possible answer: The new portable mass spectrometers are much smaller and lighter than the old ones, and they can identify the sample much more quickly.

▶ **Question 9:** Author & Me because the author explains what a mass spectrometer does, but the reader must provide an example of a real-life problem that could be solved by using a mass spectrometer. Possible answer: A real-life problem could be an accident involving a chemical spill. A mass spectrometer could be used to determine if the air is safe for people to breathe. Bring the class together and have students discuss the QAR, reasons for choosing it, and the answer for each question.

Step 5 INDEPENDENT APPLICATION

| ~~BEFORE READING~~ | DURING READING | AFTER READING |

Have students work independently to practice using QARs before, during, and after reading. Ask them to read the "Warp Drive" section and answer the following questions:

Display the following three questions:

1. How does Einstein's theory of relativity make warp speed possible?

2. In your opinion, what are the areas where researchers can come close to achieving the technology imagined on _Star Trek_? What are the areas where it appears difficult or even impossible to achieve the results imagined on _Star Trek_?

3. Is it important for scientists to try to make _Star Trek_ technology a reality? Explain your thinking.

Ask students to add these questions to their sheet of paper and continue to include the QAR, reason, and answer for each question. Tell them to be prepared to share their work.

Circulate around the room, giving students guidance as needed. QARs, reasons, and possible answers for these questions appear below.

▶ **Question 1:** Right There because the information can be found in one sentence. Possible answer: *Einstein's theory allows warp speed to be reached by squishing the space in front of an object and stretching out the space in back of it.*

▶ **Question 2:** Author & Me because the author's clues are necessary, and the question asks for the reader's opinion. Possible answer: *In my opinion, researchers are getting close to Star Trek technology with medical care and portable mass spectrometers because I have seen things sort of like this when I was at the emergency room. They are much farther away with instantaneous transport and traveling faster than the speed of light because we don't have space travel to different planets and still have to take some kind of vehicle to get from one place to another that is far away.*

▶ **Question 3:** Author & Me because the author's clues are necessary, and this question again asks for the reader's opinion. Possible answer: *I think scientists should try to make Star Trek technology a reality because this technology can make life better for people on Earth and give us the chance to explore the galaxy.*

After having a few students share their responses, reinforce the idea that the type of QARs generally found after reading are Author & Me.

Note: Author & Me is critical for deeper comprehension of a text. This QAR requires close reading, unlike On My Own, and, in contrast to Right There or Think & Search, it moves students to reflect upon the significance of the text.

Step **6** SELF-ASSESSMENT & GOAL SETTING

In preparation for having students complete their QAR Self-Assessment Thinksheet, display and revisit the I Can Statement:

I can use QARs to improve my comprehension throughout the reading cycle: before reading, during reading, and after reading.

Invite students to share what they have learned about the QAR most likely to occur during different times in the reading cycle as shown below:

▶ Before reading: On My Own, Author & Me

▶ During reading: Think & Search, Right There, Author & Me

▶ After reading: Author & Me

Remind students that knowing which QARs are likely to occur during each part of the reading cycle can help them with answering questions and comprehending the text.

> *Now I would like you to think about how you can use this strategy in other areas and how you can add this to your own personal toolkit for reading.*

Have students complete a QAR Self-Assessment Thinksheet and turn it in along with their work on the questions in the Coaching and Independent Application steps.

For use
with Step 2:
Modeling:

title, introduction,
and
illustration

Star Trek Tech

By Karina Hamalainen

How close are we to reaching 23rd-century technology? The crew from the *Starship Enterprise* lands in theaters in a prequel to the famed Star Trek series. For the first time, fans will see how James Tiberius Kirk became Captain Kirk and how the rest of the crew ended up exploring outer space together.

During their adventures, the crew members use futuristic gadgets that allow them to beam down instantly to new planets, easily examine the sick, and cross the universe at faster-than-light warp speed. How realistic are these tricked-out tools? Read on to see how today's science stacks up against the world of Star Trek.

Transporters: "Beam me up, Scotty!"

The *Starship Enterprise* crew can instantly transport themselves to a new location. They do this by breaking down their bodies into their smallest components, or atoms, and then rematerializing in the location of their choice. However, there are some major challenges with this method of travel. According to physicist Lawrence Krauss, author of *The Physics of Star Trek*, the human body is made of approximately 10 octillion (that's 10 followed by 28 zeros!) atoms. To dematerialize a person weighing 50 kilograms (110 pounds), it would take more energy than the amount contained in 1,000 hydrogen bombs.

Reconstructing a person would require an instruction manual for the transporter that described where each of those atoms goes. Krauss estimates that such a manual would contain more than 10,000 times the information in all the books ever written.

Still, some researchers remain undaunted. A team from the University of Vienna in Austria has managed to instantaneously transport individual electrons (negatively charged particles) and photons (particles of light) more than 143 kilometers (89 miles). But Krauss doesn't believe this will work on humans. "We're big, jumbled-up, complicated matter—very different from a simple electron," he says.

For use
with Step 4:
Coaching:

"Sickbay" and
"Tricorders"
sections

Sickbay: "Live long and prosper."

In the 23rd century, healing the sick is usually a breeze. Dr. "Bones" McCoy, the medical officer, takes a crew member of the *Starship Enterprise* to the Sickbay and uses scanners to quickly diagnose the patient. If he needs to, he can perform surgery with lasers or give medicine with a needle-free "hypospray" device.

Medicine is one area where we are rapidly catching up with Star Trek. Non-invasive scanners like X-rays, magnetic resonance imaging (MRI) devices, and computerized axial tomography (CAT) scans can take pictures of your insides, so a doctor can diagnose what ails you. Lasers are used to perform surgery on many body parts. And since 1985, a company named Bioject has been making devices like McCoy's hypospray. These work by using compressed air or springs to shoot out a stream of liquid medication at high speeds. The stream is so narrow and quick that it pierces the skin like a needle—minus the pain!

Tricorders: "It's life, Jim, but not like we know it . . . "

After beaming down onto an unexplored planet, crew members want to know if it is safe to check out. A handheld device called a "tricorder" allows crew members to scan the environment for harmful compounds in the air or lurking alien life-forms.

Last year [2008], researchers at Purdue University in West Lafayette, Indiana, made a tricorder-like portable mass spectrometer. This device can identify chemical compounds and measure their amounts in the air. Normally, mass spectrometers weigh hundreds of pounds, and the analysis takes a long time before it yields results. But scientists have been able to shrink the device down to the size of a large lunchbox. "That's batteries and everything," says R. Graham Cooks, leader of the Purdue research team. Once the air sample is taken, the data are transferred wirelessly to a computer that identifies the sample in fewer than five seconds. Cooks envisions a day when this device is used anywhere that chemical analysis needs to be done—maybe even on a faraway planet.

Warp Drive: "Space, the final frontier . . ."

For use with
Step 3: Guided
Practice:

"Warp Drive"
section

Warp speed allows the *Starship Enterprise* to go faster than the speed of light, which is 300,000 km (186,411 mi) per second. So it takes the crew only hours to make trips that would normally take thousands of years. This enables the *Starship Enterprise* to travel deep into the galaxy.

Will we ever be able to go faster than the speed of light? "It's possible in theory," says author and physicist Krauss. Albert Einstein's theory of general relativity describes how space and time warp (bend) due to gravity (force of attraction between objects). His theory allows for warp speed to be accomplished by squishing the space in front of an object, like the *Starship Enterprise*, and stretching the space behind it. That way the object has to move only a few feet instead of a few light-years (distance light travels in one year, roughly equal to 9.5 trillion kilometers, or 5.9 trillion miles). But, as with the transporter, traveling at warp speed would take a lot of energy.

Will we ever invent a warp drive that can bend space? Maybe your generation will find a way to overcome these technological hurdles. We still have 200 years to overcome all of these challenges before the *Starship Enterprise* and her crew embark on their 23rd-century mission: "To boldly go where no man has gone before."

Predicting With Informational Text

GOAL ●
Help students understand how making predictions before and during reading can enhance comprehension

I Can Statement

I can make predictions and check them for accuracy by using the QAR Author & Me Prediction Chart.

Reading Cycle & QAR:

Reading Cycle: Before and During Reading

QAR: *Author & Me:* Using author's clues to identify useful background knowledge and experiences

Materials *(See CD for reproducibles.)*

▶ "Ingredients for a Good Hair Day" by Joe Levitt (informational passage), p. 45 (display copy, one copy for each student)

▶ The Core QARs Poster and QAR and the Reading Cycle Poster (display copy of each)

▶ QAR Author & Me Prediction Chart (display copy, one copy for each student)

▶ highlighter

▶ QAR Self-Assessment Thinksheet (one copy for each student)

BEFORE READING	DURING READING	AFTER READING

Step 1 EXPLICIT EXPLANATION

Let students know that the focus of this lesson is on prediction, an important comprehension strategy used before and during reading.

Today we will be learning about how we make predictions before and during reading. Before and during reading informational text, good readers constantly ask themselves the question, "What do I think is going to be discussed next in this text?" These predictions get us ready to make sense of what we are reading, especially if the text is complicated. The QAR is Author & Me because we need clues from the author to identify the In My Head information that can help us make reasonable predictions. We will learn how to use the QAR Author & Me Prediction Chart to keep track of In the Book information, In My Head information, and the predictions we create. Today we'll be making predictions about the passage "Ingredients for a Good Hair Day."

Step 2 MODELING

Display the QAR Author & Me Prediction Chart. Reiterate that you will be using this chart to help you make good predictions. Go over the heading for each column: Author (In the Book information), Me (In My Head information), Prediction (comprehension strategy), and Notes.

To make a prediction, I need to use information the author gives me and my own background knowledge and experiences to think about what I know that is relevant to the text. So, prediction is an Author & Me QAR. I ask myself the question, "What do I think will happen next?" Notice the first column heading: Author. This is where I record the author's clues in the text. The second column heading, Me, is where I record my own relevant knowledge and experiences. The third column, Prediction, puts the Author & Me QAR together. I am working with the author to figure out what might happen next, using clues in the text and information I already know. I use the fourth column, Notes, during reading. Making notes helps me keep track of whether my previous predictions were correct and when I might need to think about drawing on different background knowledge and experiences or changing my original prediction.

Once you feel students understand the connection to QAR language, model how to use the QAR Author & Me Prediction Chart to develop good predictions.

The passage today is from the magazine Science World. *The title is "Ingredients for a Good Hair Day." Before reading, I want to think about the author's clues that I can gather from the title and whether I have any background knowledge or experiences that will help me understand the passage better as I read. Since this passage is an article from a magazine called* Science World*, this gives me a clue about the genre of text. I think the passage will contain scientific information.*

The first word in the title is "ingredients." I'm going to write this word in the Author column since this is what the author has written In the Book. I know ingredients can be everything that goes into a product or recipe, such as soup or a cake. This information comes from In My Head, so I'm going to write it in the Me column. The next part of the title is "good hair day," and I'm going to write this in the Author column. Ah! I wish every day were a good hair day! A good hair day for me is when my hair does what I want it to, when it's not frizzy or tangled. There are many hair-care products that can make hair look good. I am going to write this information in the Me column. Starting with the author's information and adding my own knowledge, I predict that the article will explain how certain ingredients in hair-care products can help our hair look good. I'll write my prediction in the Prediction column.

QAR Author & Me Prediction Chart

AUTHOR	ME	PREDICTION	NOTES
• ingredients	• what a product or food is made of	The article will explain how certain ingredients in hair-care products can help our hair look good.	(add notes after reading up to stop sign 1) accurate: "bad hair day now and then" "many hair care products" "shampoo and conditioner"
• good hair day	• Hair-care products can make hair look good.		

Explain that you're going to read the first two paragraphs of the passage aloud to see if you can confirm or add to your prediction. Point out the stop sign and indicate that this tells you when to stop reading and make your prediction. After reading this section aloud, model your use of text information to confirm your prediction. As you speak, underline the author's clues that confirm your prediction. Some relevant text examples include the following: "everyone has a bad hair day now and then"; "many hair-care products claim to tame unruly tresses"; "long list of ingredients on your shampoo and conditioner bottles"; "pops the lid on hair-care products to find out."

After reading the first two paragraphs and stopping when I came to the stop sign, I can see that my prediction is correct. The passage will explain how certain ingredients in hair-care products can help our hair. Because my prediction is accurate, I'm going to go back to the Notes column and write "accurate." I'm also going to add text clues that prove that my prediction is accurate. Had my prediction been incorrect, I would have written "inaccurate" and added relevant text clues. I would then revise my prediction based on these new clues. Sometimes, the author doesn't address the predictions we've made. In that situation, I would write "not addressed" in the Notes column.

Step 3 GUIDED PRACTICE

Distribute a copy of the passage to each student. Tell them that now you'll work together to practice using the QAR Author & Me Prediction Chart for making and refining predictions, following the same steps you just modeled.

Ask students to read the subtitle with you: "Hair Basics."

I want you to help me think about the information we can add to each column in the chart based on this new author clue, "Hair Basics." Think about clues from the author, your own background knowledge, and possible predictions.

Call on students to share their ideas and enter them in the chart. After completing the first three columns of the chart, direct students to continue to read to stop sign 3. Work with students to check the prediction on the class chart. Complete the Notes column indicating "accurate," "inaccurate," or "not addressed" and relevant author's clues. Sample entries for the chart appear below.

AUTHOR	ME	PREDICTION	NOTES
• hair • basics	• Most people have hair on their heads. • simple, easy, breaking something down	This section of the article will explain simple things about our hair.	(add after reading to stop sign 3) accurate: "understand a little bit about your hair"

Students should complete the prediction cycle based on the heading and their reading of the first two paragraphs. Remind them that they should underline clues from the author and think about their own relevant ideas. Then ask students to predict what might happen next, using the author's clues from this section (to stop sign 3) and their own ideas. Enter their suggestions in the chart, including their prediction for the remainder of the section.

Then read aloud the last two paragraphs of this section (up to stop sign 4) and work with students to underline relevant author clues. Complete the Notes column with "accurate," "inaccurate," or "not addressed" and include relevant author's clues.

The sample below will help you get started.

AUTHOR	ME	PREDICTION	NOTES
Too much sebum can cause your hair to be a matted mess.	If my body makes too much sebum, there has to be something I can do to keep my hair from becoming tangled, frizzy, and matted.	This portion of the article will tell me what I can do to keep my hair from tangling and being a mess.	(add after reading to stop sign 4) accurate: "Taking a shower is part of the solution, but water alone won't wash away the filth . . . that's where shampoo comes in."

Note: Seek to move students away from focusing on getting the right answer to thinking in a logical manner. Be sure to praise those who show logical thinking, even if their predictions do not turn out to be accurate.

Step 4 COACHING

Distribute a blank copy of the QAR Author & Me Prediction Chart to each student or have students draw their own chart on a sheet of paper.

> *Work with a partner to read the next section, "Label Decoder." Take turns reading the text to each other. When you come to stop sign 5, stop and discuss author clues and your own knowledge that will help you create a prediction. Following their discussion, each of you should enter information in the Author, Me, and Prediction columns of your QAR Author & Me Prediction Chart before reading on. Remember that you are asking yourself, "What do I think is going to be discussed next in this article?" The QAR for this question is Author & Me, which reminds you to use clues from the author to help you identify useful In My Head information. After you have entered your prediction, read the rest of "Label Decoder" and add information to your Notes column—"accurate," "inaccurate," or "not addressed"—as well as relevant author's clues.*

Circulate to observe your students' thinking. If you notice students who have completed all four columns of their chart, invite them to add their entries to the class chart.

A sample chart entry for this portion of the text appears below.

AUTHOR	ME	PREDICTION	NOTES
• label • decoder	• Labels describe what's inside something. • Decoding is when you figure something out.	The information will tell us what the labels on hair products mean so we can tell what ingredients are in them and what each one does.	(add after reading to stop sign 6) accurate: "Ammonium Laureth Sulfate: Detergent that removes oils."

Step 5 INDEPENDENT APPLICATION

> *Read the last two sections of the passages, "Squeaky Clean" and "Protective Powers," on your own. As you read, keep asking yourself, "What do I think is going to be discussed next in this text?" When you get to the first stop sign in this section, stop and enter information in the Author, Me, and Prediction columns of the QAR Author & Me Prediction Chart before reading on. When you get to the next stop sign, go back and check your last prediction and fill in the Notes column. Then add your next prediction to your chart. Continue doing this until you have read the entire article and you have made and checked all your predictions.*

Invite a few students to add their entries to the class chart. Then call the whole group back together and ask several students to share entries from their charts. A sample chart entry for the final portion of the text appears below.

AUTHOR	ME	PREDICTION	NOTES
• squeaky clean • These detergents remove dirt in a clever way.	• I use shampoo to get my hair clean. • I know detergents remove oil from reading about it in the previous section.	I think this section of the text will talk about how shampoos are made and how they work to clean hair.	(Add after reading to stop sign 8) accurate: "Sebum and waxy materials are dissolved by the detergent." "Oils and dirt are washed down the drain."
• necessitating a squirt of artificial conditioner • protective powers	• makes hair soft • to protect is to shield or defend control	I think this section will be about how conditioner works to protect and control hair.	(add after reading to stop sign 10) accurate: "Chemicals coat damaged hair shafts in order to protect them."
• finding ways to improve the look and feel of your locks • bits of insight that improve the product	• to discover through research • to make something better	The end of the article might talk about research being done to make hair-care products better.	(add after reading to stop sign 11) accurate" "research organization" "Bad hair will one day be a thing of the past."

As students share, guide them to the understanding that using In the Book clues to identify useful In My Head information can lead them to make sound predictions.

AFTER READING

Step **6** SELF-ASSESSMENT & GOAL-SETTING

Display the I Can Statement and read it aloud. Then connect it to the lesson.

> *The purpose of this lesson is to help you learn to use predictions before and during reading to improve your comprehension of the text. We learned to make predictions and check them by using the QAR Author & Me Prediction Chart.*

Call on volunteers to explain how they used the QAR Author & Me Prediction Chart to make and check predictions.

> *Now I would like you to think about how you can use the strategy of prediction in other areas, and how you can add prediction to your own personal toolkit for reading.*

Then have students complete a thinksheet and turn it in with their complete chart.

Ingredients for a Good Hair Day

By Joe Levitt

For use with Step 2: Modeling: title, first 2 paragraphs

Fed up with horrible hair? Chemistry can come to your rescue.

Everyone has a bad hair day now and then. From frizz to flyaways, unkempt locks can lower your self-esteem and get you down. Many hair-care products claim to tame unruly tresses. But what does the long list of ingredients on your shampoo and conditioner bottles really do for your hair? *Science World* pops the lid on hair-care products to find out. **1**

Hair Basics **2**

For use with Step 3: Guided Practice: "Hair Basics" section

To create the look you want, first you need to understand a little about your hair. Strands of hair grow within the lower layer of your skin in structures called follicles. There, glands pump out sebum. Think of this oily substance as your body's natural hair conditioner.

Sebum helps to waterproof your hair and keep your scalp moist. But too much can cause your hair to become a matted mess. **3**

"Picture what would happen to your table top if you treated it with just plain wax," says Mort Westman, a cosmetic chemist at the cosmetics research and development firm Westman Associates in Oak Brook, Illinois. "Every bit of dust and dirt that flew by or was electrically attracted to the table would become stuck and remain in place. The same thing happens to hair."

Taking a shower is part of the solution, but water alone won't wash away the filth. That's because water is a polar molecule, which means it has a slightly positive end and a slightly negative end. Sebum, like other oils, is nonpolar. This type of compound does not dissolve well in water. That's where shampoo comes in. **4**

Label Decoder **5**

For use with Step 4: Coaching: "Label Decoder" section

Here's a rundown of some common shampoo ingredients and their purposes.

- WATER: Keeps other ingredients well mixed throughout
- AMMONIUM LAURETH SULFATE: Detergent that removes oils
- DIMETHICONE: Lubricates, smoothes, and adds shine to dry hair
- XANTHAN GUM: Thickens the product/formula
- CETYL ALCOHOL AND STEARYL ALCOHOL: Thickens formula and lubricates hair
- DISODIUM EDTA: Removes unwanted metals from water and makes preservatives more efficient
- COCAMIDE DEA: Modifies foam so it lasts longer
- GLYCERINE: Keeps formula uniform **6**

Squeaky Clean

For use with Step 5: Independent Application: "Squeaky Clean" and "Protective Powers" sections

Look on a list of shampoo ingredients, and you'll see chemicals like sodium lauryl sulfate and cocamidopropyl betaine. These detergents remove dirt in a clever way. **7**

"The function of a detergent is to 'marry' oil-soluble materials with water-soluble materials," says Westman. A detergent is a long molecule with one polar end and one nonpolar end, he explains. Sebum and waxy materials are dissolved by the detergent's nonpolar end and are swept into the water by its polar end. Thus oils and dirt are washed down the drain even though they are only indirectly attached to the water molecules. But there's a catch: Shampoos strip away the scalp's naturally protective sebum, necessitating a squirt of artificial conditioner. **8**

Protective Powers **9**

Scientists cook up conditioners to help out hair in two ways. One way uses a mixture of positively charged molecules often listed on the bottle as amodimethicone, distearyldimonium chloride, and cetrimonium chloride. These chemicals coat damaged hair shafts in order to protect them.

A second way conditioners are helpful is that they sometimes contain suspended microdroplets of silicone. This is especially true of 2-in-1 shampoo/conditioner products. The silicones smooth and lubricate the surface of the hairs, which gives them shine and keeps them from intertwining. Hairs tangle because their outer surface, the cuticle, becomes rough from damage, and grabs onto the hairs' neighbors.

Although hair-care products have been around for a long time, industry experts are still finding ways to help improve the look and feel of your locks. "As companies tinker with chemicals, they gain little bits of insight that improve the product. **10**

The next generation of shampoos and conditioners will be better than the current one," says Peter Kaplan, research director at the product testing and research organization TRI/Princeton in New Jersey. With any luck, bad hair days will one day be a thing of the past. **11**

Predicting With Narrative Text

GOAL • Help students understand how making predictions before and during reading can enhance comprehension

I Can Statement

I can make predictions and check them for accuracy by using the QAR Author & Me T-Chart.

Reading Cycle & QARs

Reading Cycle: Before and During Reading

QAR: *Author & Me:* Using author's clues to identify useful background knowledge and experiences

Materials *(See CD for reproducibles.)*

▶ "A Legend of the Knights of the Round Table" (narrative selection), p. 51 (display copy, one copy for each student)

▶ The Core QARs Poster and QAR and the Reading Cycle Poster (display copy of each)

▶ QAR Author & Me T-Chart (display copy, one copy for each student)

▶ QAR Self-Assessment Thinksheet (one copy for each student)

BEFORE READING DURING READING AFTER READING

Step 1 EXPLICIT EXPLANATION

Tell students that the purpose of today's lesson is to learn to use the QAR Author & Me T-Chart to help make predictions with narrative text and to determine the accuracy of these predictions. To make predictions, they will start with clues from the author to figure out which part of their background knowledge and experiences to draw on in formulating their predictions. They will then use information from the text to determine the degree to which their predictions are supported.

Review and expand on what students learned in Lesson 5. Focus on the following points: First, predictions are Author & Me QARs that ask about what comes next in the reading. For narrative text, the prediction is generally about upcoming events in a story. In this lesson, students will build on what they learned about the QAR Author & Me Prediction Chart using a new tool, the QAR Author & Me T-Chart. Explain that this chart is slightly simpler than the prediction chart, but it requires the same level of thinking about author's clues and the reader's own knowledge to make a prediction that helps with comprehension.

Good readers strengthen their comprehension by making predictions before and during reading. When I read, I use clues from the author to think about how accurate my predictions have been. If a prediction isn't supported, then I use the text information to revise my thinking.

BEFORE READING **DURING READING** AFTER READING

Step **2** MODELING

Display the QAR Author & Me T-Chart and explain that this new tool will help students develop predictions and record information about the accuracy of their predictions.

QAR Author & Me T-Chart

PREDICTIONS	TEXT EVIDENCE

Predicting helps focus my attention during reading because I can read to see if the author's words support, or fail to support, my predictions. The QAR Author & Me T-Chart will help me organize the evidence in the text that I will use to test my prediction for accuracy.

Display the passage, "A Legend of the Knights of the Round Table." Explain that you will write your predictions about this passage in the Predictions column of the QAR Author & Me T-Chart and then add notes from the text in the Text Evidence column. Samples of useful information to include in each column are underlined below. Let students know that you will be checking your predictions for accuracy, modifying your predictions, and creating new predictions when it's necessary.

I'll start by thinking about the title since that is often the author's first clue. "A Legend of the Knights of the Round Table" does give me some useful information. I know that a legend is a story from long ago and that legends usually describe someone heroic. Even when a legend is based on the life of a real person and something he or she has done, over time, the story gets exaggerated and becomes a mixture of fact and fiction, so I'm already predicting this narrative <u>text is a story about someone heroic</u>.

The next part of the title is "Knights of the Round Table." I've read about knights before, and I've seen them portrayed in movies. I know knights are like soldiers who lived in medieval times and who protected people in danger. I'm not sure what the round table stands for, so I am not going to use that in my prediction. But the clues make me think that this will be a story about <u>soldiers from medieval times who do some things that help others</u>.

Explain that as you read you will be looking for clues in the text that either support, or fail to support, your predictions. Checking to see if your predictions are accurate or inaccurate helps you make sure that you are making sense of the text and deciding if, or how, you need to rethink your ideas.

Read aloud the first paragraph and have students follow along on the display copy. As you read aloud, jot down information in the Text Evidence column on the chart. Include information such as the following: more than 1000 years ago, brave knights, something extraordinary happened.

> *The author's clues help me test my prediction. The story takes place a long time ago, is about brave knights, and is going to describe something extraordinary. My prediction is holding up, so I know that so far I'm on track in understanding the story. However, if there had been no text evidence to support my prediction, I would have needed to modify my prediction based on the author's clues. As I read on, I will keep using text clues to create new predictions that I can test as I read.*

Step **3** GUIDED PRACTICE

Provide each student with a copy of the passage. Ask them to follow along as you read the next section of the passage, underlining text evidence that relates to the current predictions in the chart. Have two or three students share the evidence they noted. Record their ideas in the Text Evidence column of the class chart. Phrases such as knights are the bravest in the world and any knight here is brave enough support the prediction that the text describes something spectacular that might happen, as do the exaggerated descriptions of a green knight (e.g., Everything was green: face, armor, horse).

Shift to the creation of a new prediction by drawing students' attention to the Green Knight's carrying a massive ax and requesting that a brave knight strike him with it.

> *The Green Knight may do something spectacular or perhaps something terrible. I think a new prediction about the Green Knight will be useful for checking my comprehension as I read.*

Invite students to create a prediction that has something to do with the Green Knight. Then call on a few students to share examples and add them to the class chart. Tell students that they will use these predictions, as well as others they may have in mind that are not on the class chart, in the next part of the lesson.

Predictions may include, but are not limited to, the following:

- ▶ The Knights of the Round Table will refuse to swing the ax.
- ▶ A Round Table Knight will volunteer to swing the ax.
- ▶ The Green Knight will trick the Round Table Knight who volunteers and will kill him.

Step 4 COACHING

Distribute a copy of the blank QAR Author & Me T-Chart to each student, or have everyone draw their own T-chart on a sheet of paper. Ask partners to work together to read the section, check their predictions about the Green Knight, and make predictions about the next section. Students should work together to discuss the text but record their own predictions and text information on individual T-charts. Tell pairs to identify at least two predictions about the next section of text. They may choose from their own predictions about the Green Knight as well as from predictions on the class T-chart. Once partners have agreed on the predictions, they should read the text together and underline clues that provide evidence to confirm or disprove their prediction. Pairs should discuss the evidence they've underlined and enter relevant text clues in the Text Evidence column of their T-charts. They should end this part of their work by creating a new prediction to guide their reading of the final section of the text.

Confirming or disproving text evidence will vary depending on the prediction. Potential evidence in this section of the text includes the following: "ask for your own death"; Green Knight changes the rules so he can strike back; "no man has ever survived a blow" from Knight Gawain; promise to go to the Green Knight's castle so he can strike Gawain; Green Knight remains alive after his head is chopped off; Green Knight reminds Gawain of his promise.

As pairs work, circulate around the room to provide assistance as needed. When students are finished, ask several pairs to share their text clues for the prediction about the Green Knight and their new prediction for the next section. Enter the evidence that students identified to support or disprove earlier predictions in the Text Evidence column of the class chart. Add students' new and revised predictions to the chart. Remind them that their predictions keep them focused on key ideas in the story and help deepen their comprehension.

Step 5 INDEPENDENT APPLICATION

Explain to students that they will now be making and checking predictions on their own, using the individual QAR Author & Me T-Chart they started earlier.

> *Make your final predictions for the remainder of the text. You may create your own predictions based on what we have read so far, as well as draw on those you and your partner created or those in the class chart. Read the rest of the story and use the author's clues to determine how well your prediction is supported and where new text clues might have surprised you.*

Then ask for volunteers to share their predictions, relevant information from the author, and whether their predictions were supported by the text. Encourage students to discuss the information from the author that supported, or failed to support, their predictions.

Possible predictions for the last section include the following: Sir Gawain will kill the Green Knight; Sir Gawain will trick the Green Knight and escape having to battle him; the Green Knight kills Gawain, but Gawain shows he is honorable and brave. Key evidence in the last section includes the following: Gawain kept his promise; the Green Knight was sent to test Gawain's bravery, not to kill him. Gawain is the bravest of all knights ("has no equal").

Step **6** SELF-ASSESSMENT & GOAL-SETTING

Display the I Can Statement and ask students to keep it in mind as they think about what they have learned. Have them turn to a partner and describe what they learned about creating and testing predictions, and how that helped them deepen their understanding of the passage. Elicit several student responses, reinforcing the idea that the QAR Author & Me T-Chart helped them comprehend text by using predictions to focus their reading and keeping track of evidence to confirm or disprove their predictions. Point out that as they read, active readers are constantly checking their understanding against the new clues the author provides. Remind students that predictions will vary among readers and that the goal is not to generate the right prediction, but rather to use their predictions to help them understand the texts they read.

Conclude the lesson by having students discuss the general usefulness of making predictions.

> *Think about how you can use the strategy of making predictions in other areas and how you can add this strategy to your personal toolkit for reading.*

Ask students to complete the QAR Self-Assessment Thinksheet and turn it in with their completed QAR Author & Me T-Chart.

A Legend of the Knights of the Round Table

For use with Step 2: Modeling: title and first 2 paragraphs

Old legends tell us that more than 1,000 years ago, England had a king named Arthur. King Arthur had a group of brave knights. They were known as the Knights of the Round Table.

Every Christmas, the Knights of the Round Table came together. They feasted and told about their adventures. One year during their feast, something extraordinary happened.

◆ ◆ ◆

For use with Step 3: Guided Practice: next 6 paragraphs

The Knights of the Round Table were laughing and telling stories when all of a sudden the palace's heavy door swung open. In the doorway, mounted on a huge horse, was a green knight. Everything about him was green: his face, his armor, even his horse; and he carried a massive green ax.

"Which of you is King Arthur?" he asked.

The king stood up. "I am Arthur," he said.

"I have heard that your knights are the bravest in the world," said the Green Knight. "I want to know which of you is brave enough to do what I ask."

"Any knight here is brave enough," King Arthur said. "What is it that you ask?"

The Green Knight got off his horse, cleared his throat, held up his ax, and then spoke. "I want a knight to take this ax and strike me with it."

◆ ◆ ◆

For use with Step 4: Coaching: next 12 paragraphs

The room was silent.

"Are you all cowards?" he roared.

King Arthur spoke, "Sir, what you ask for makes no sense. You ask for your own death."

The Green Knight laughed.

A knight named Sir Gawain stepped forward. Gawain said, "No one laughs at the Knights of the Round Table. Hand me that ax, and I will strike your laughing head from your body!"

Gawain took the ax from the Green Knight and got ready to swing. "Just a minute," the Green Knight said. "This has to be fair. In return for striking me, I have the right to strike you back."

"You have the right, yes," said Gawain. "But no man has ever survived a blow from me."

"We shall see," said the Green Knight. "You must promise to come to my castle a year from now. Then, I will hold the ax and I will strike you with it."

Gawain smiled, knowing that day would never come. "It will be as you wish. I promise," he said.

The Green Knight lifted his long green hair to expose his green neck. Gawain swung the ax and struck the Green Knight's neck, cutting his head clear off his body. The Green Knight's head bounced and rolled on the floor.

Oddly, the Green Knight's body did not fall. With his arms, he simply reached down and picked up his own rolling head by its green hair.

The Green Knight held his head in front of him. His lips smiled a cruel smile as the Green Knight started to speak. "Do not forget your promise. In one year, at my Green Castle in the North Country, meet me and accept your fate."

For use with Step 5: Independent Application:

remainder of story

A year later Gawain kept his promise.

Sir Gawain led his horse through the snow in the North Country until he found a castle. The lord of the castle, Lord Westall, helped Gawain into a chair by a warm fire. Lady Westall sat nearby.

Gawain asked Lord Westall about the Green Castle. "It is just an hour from here," Lord Westall said. "But they say a monster, some sort of Green Knight, kills everyone who goes near it."

Sir Gawain told the lord and lady about the promise he'd made to the Green Knight. "Are you sure you want to do this?" Lord Westall asked.

Gawain nodded.

"Very well. Sleep here tonight," the lord said.

The next morning, Lady Westall walked into Sir Gawain's room and woke him. "You must escape right now," she whispered. "I will help you."

"Thank you, but I have never broken a promise," Sir Gawain said.

"Run!" the lady pleaded. "You're going to die!"

"No, I must go to the Green Castle," he said.

Gawain rode to the Green Castle and shouted at its walls: "I have come to keep my promise!"

The door opened. Out stepped the Green Knight. He held the ax. "Are you ready?" he asked.

Gawain didn't have time to answer. The Green Knight was already swinging the ax. Gawain closed his eyes. The Green Knight struck.

Gawain blinked. "What happened?" he wondered. "Am I still alive?" He turned his head from side to side. He felt his neck. The ax had stopped just as it cut the skin!

"Gawain, you have passed every test of a man who calls himself a knight," said the Green Knight. "Take a closer look at me. Do you know who I am?"

"That's right. I'm your host from last night," said the Green Knight. "I have put you through every test of bravery. You were brave in the face of death. You kept your promise, even when my wife wanted you to run away."

"But why? Who are you?" asked Sir Gawain.

"Ask not who I am, Sir Gawain," said the Green Knight. "Ask not why my skin is now green. Know only that I am the Green Knight—sent to test you, the bravest knight who has no equal."

Drawing Inferences With Informational Text

GOAL • Help students understand how drawing inferences before and during reading can enhance comprehension of informational text

I Can Statement

I can draw inferences to enhance my comprehension by using the QAR Author & Me Inference Chart.

Reading Cycle and QARs

Reading Cycle: During and After Reading

QAR: *Author & Me:* Using author's clues to identify useful background knowledge and experiences for comprehending informational text

Materials *(See CD for reproducibles.)*

▶ "Meeting Nelson Mandela" by Rebecca Leon (informational passage: biography), p. 59 (display copy, one copy for each student)

▶ The Core QARs Poster and QAR and the Reading Cycle Poster (display copy of each)

▶ QAR Author & Me Inference Chart (display copy, one copy for each student)

▶ highlighter

▶ QAR Self-Assessment Thinksheet

BEFORE READING   DURING READING   AFTER READING

Step 1 EXPLICIT EXPLANATION

Display the posters and refer to them as necessary during the lesson. Let students know that the focus of this lesson is on drawing inferences, an important comprehension strategy used during and after reading all kinds of texts, including stories, poems, and informational text.

Today we will be learning about how to draw inferences during and after reading a biography. Drawing inferences is something active readers do when they read, as

well as when they answer Author & Me questions. When I make an inference, it is like answering an Author & Me QAR. I start with the author's clues and consider whether I have any background knowledge or experiences that will help me understand the text better as I read. Authors cannot put every detail I need or want to know in the text, so I need to draw inferences to fill in those gaps.

DURING READING

Step **2** MODELING

Display The Core QARs Poster and the QAR Author & Me Inference Chart.

As they think about the clues the author gives, active readers are always asking themselves, "What background knowledge and experiences do I have that can help me understand the text?" We'll be focusing on the Author & Me QAR as we draw inferences. The QAR Author & Me Inference Chart will help us keep track of In the Book information, In My Head information, and the inferences we draw while reading.

Note: Skip the first sentence below if students have not yet participated in Lessons 5 and 6.

Notice that the QAR Author & Me Inference Chart is similar to the QAR Author & Me Prediction Chart, which you already know how to use.

Note: A prediction is essentially a before-reading inference.

In the Author column, I record the author's clues that are In the Book. In the Me column, I record my own relevant knowledge and experiences. In the Inferences column, I write the inference that I create using information from In My Head to expand on the information from In the Book.

Once you feel students understand the connection to the QAR language, model how to use the QAR Author & Me Inference Chart to draw relevant inferences.

I'll use the QAR Author & Me Inference Chart to keep track of information and to draw inferences as I go along. Today we are going to read a passage called "Meeting Nelson Mandela." The title gives me my first clues from the author, so I'll write it in the Author column. Right away, I activate my background knowledge about Nelson Mandela. I've seen him on TV and read about him in the newspaper, and I know he was a great leader in South Africa.

The word "meeting" in the title makes me wonder if I will "meet" Nelson Mandela through the author's words or if someone will actually meet him in person. I'll add this information to the Me column of the chart. My inference is that someone will get to meet Nelson Mandela. I think that is a reasonable inference because that someone could be someone in the story, or it could be the reader. I will add that to the Inference column.

Display and read aloud the first paragraph of the passage. Underline relevant text clues as you read and think aloud as shown below.

In the first paragraph, I learn that <u>Stephanie Chung</u> is a <u>16-year-old</u> who wrote an <u>award-winning essay</u> about <u>Nelson Mandela</u>. Since these are all clues from In the Book, I am going to add them to the Author column in my chart. When I was in high school, I remember writing essays for my classes all the time. I'm going to write this background knowledge in the Me column. Starting with the author's information, and using my own knowledge, my inference right now is that the girl, Stephanie, wrote her essay about Nelson Mandela for a school essay-writing contest.

Possible entries are in the chart below.

QAR Author & Me Inference Chart

AUTHOR	ME	INFERENCE
• "Meeting" Nelson Mandela	• great leader in South Africa • meeting through the author's words or meeting in person?	• Someone will meet Nelson Mandela.
• Stephanie Chung writes award winning essay.	• Essays are assigned in school.	• for school contest

Display and read aloud the second paragraph.

Now that I've read this paragraph, I see why Stephanie wrote the essay! It was for a competition, sponsored by the Nelson Mandela Foundation.

Cross out <u>for school contest</u> in the third column and add <u>competition sponsored by Mandela Foundation</u>.

As I read on, I gained new clues from In the Book, which helped me realize that my inference was reasonable but incorrect. When I first make an inference, I don't worry about whether it is "right" because I can easily revise it when the author provides me with more information.

Step 3 GUIDED PRACTICE

Display the next section of the passage, "Fighting for Equality." Distribute one copy of the passage to each student. Tell students that you will now guide them in using the QAR Author & Me Inference Chart to draw relevant inferences, following the same steps you just modeled. Have them follow along as you read the section. As you read, underline author's clues that initiate your thinking about what you already know that is relevant to the text.

In the first sentence, the author tells us that <u>Nelson Mandela led a 30-year struggle to end segregation in South Africa</u>. I can write these important clues in the Author column of our chart. What In My Head background knowledge or experiences can you add to these In the Book author's clues?

Call on a few students to share their responses and add their ideas to the Me column.

> *Look at the chart. What would be a reasonable inference to make, given the author's clues and your own knowledge and experiences?*

Record suggestions from several students in the third column. Have them explain the logic underlying their inferences. Emphasize that the idea is to make inferences that seem reasonable, given the information already in the first and second columns.

Continue working with students to find relevant author's clues in the "Fighting for Equality" section. Guide students to use the author's clues to initiate background knowledge and then draw relevant inferences by putting the QAR together. Enter their suggestions in the appropriate columns of the QAR Author & Me Inference Chart.

Note: Two examples will suffice if students have grasped the strategy. Use more examples only if students will benefit from further guidance.

If you read author's clues that support or disprove previous inferences, go back and revise the inferences as appropriate to reflect the In the Book information now available. Sample responses are shown below.

AUTHOR	ME	INFERENCE
• Nelson Mandela led a 30-year struggle to end segregation in South Africa.	• A 30-year struggle is a long time. • It took a long time to end segregation here in America. • Segregation means "to be separated."	• Nelson Mandela is strong, faithful, hardworking, confident. • Fighting for segregation was not easy.
• White minority held power over black majority. • Black majority could not vote or leave home without an ID card.	• Inequality is not fair. • I would feel mistreated if I did not have the same rights as everyone else.	• The black citizens must have been sad and angry about the unfair treatment.
• Offered freedom if he stopped fighting apartheid • He refused—and remained in jail.	• I would have taken the offer and gone home because I would have missed my family and my freedom.	• Nelson Mandela was not a selfish man. He put his country before himself.

Note: Seek to move students away from focusing on getting the right answer to thinking in a logical manner. Be sure to praise those who show logical thinking, even if their inferences do not turn out to be accurate.

Step 4 COACHING

Distribute a blank copy of the QAR Author & Me Inference Chart to each student or have them draw their own charts on the top half of a sheet of notebook paper.

> *You will now be working with a partner to read the sections "Changes and Challenges" and "An Inspiring Moment." Take turns reading the text to each other. As you read, underline author's clues that trigger your background knowledge and experiences. Each of you should enter information into the Author, Me, and Inference columns on your own chart.*

Remind students who are experiencing difficulty to ask themselves the following question to guide their thinking: Building on the author's clues, what background knowledge or experiences can I use to help me understand the text?

Have two pairs of students form squares of four to share their work. As they pair-share, they should exchange the inferences they drew, explaining why these inferences are logical and useful in understanding the text. Afterward, call on a few pairs to share and add their information to the class chart. Praise students who show logical thinking. A sample chart entry for this section of the text appears below.

AUTHOR	ME	INFERENCE
• Principles of equality are written in South Africa's constitution.	• The U.S. Constitution also promises equality for all mankind, but things aren't equal. There are still a lot of inequalities.	• Even though apartheid ended, everyone probably doesn't have equal rights; it will take time before South Africans see more equality in their society.
• face tough challenges; high unemployment and crime	• The United States just went through a recession. There's a lot of crime in some cities.	• No matter what happens, there will always be unemployment and crime.
• Jeniffer said, "Why couldn't I give a voice and a face to victims all around the world?"	• Giving a voice to someone means that you'll speak out for others, to protect victims.	• As an adult, Jeniffer might be a social justice activist. She will serve the people of her country in a positive way.

Step 5 INDEPENDENT APPLICATION

Tell students they will now be working independently on their individual QAR Author & Me Inference Chart.

> *On your own, please read the final section, "Making Changes Together." As you read, remember to start with the author's clues, then see if you have any*

useful background knowledge that can help you draw an inference to further your understanding of the text. Complete all three columns in your QAR Author & Me Inference Chart to draw at least two inferences.

Encourage students who finish early to add more entries to their chart. Invite a few students to add their entries to the class chart. Then call the whole group back together and ask some students to share entries from their charts, inferences, and the logic behind these inferences.

A sample chart entry for the final section appears below.

AUTHOR	ME	INFERENCE
• Mandela Day to establish Mandela's birthday as a day of action • Mandela said, "live in a way that respects and enhances the freedom of others."	• In the U.S. we celebrate Martin Luther King, Jr.'s birthday. • MLK Jr.'s speech "I Have a Dream" is a well-known and often recited speech.	• Nelson Mandela is to South Africa what Martin Luther King, Jr. is to America.
• Mandela raised the bar for us, and now we have to reach, or even exceed, his standards.	• People always told me I was a good writer, and it raised the bar for me—it made me want to be a better writer.	• If students win this award, it will most likely change their lives by making them want to do more for others/follow in Mandela's footsteps.

AFTER READING

Step **6** SELF-ASSESSMENT & GOAL-SETTING

Display the I Can Statement and read it aloud. Connect it to this lesson.

> *The purpose of this lesson was to help you learn to draw inferences during and after reading to improve your comprehension of a text. We learned to draw inferences by using the QAR Author & Me Inference Chart. Who can explain how using the chart helped us draw relevant inferences and comprehend what we read?*

Call on two or three volunteers to explain how they used the QAR Author & Me Inference Chart to draw inferences.

> *Now I would like you to think about how you can use the strategy of drawing inferences in other areas and how you can add inferences to your own personal toolkit for reading.*

Have students complete a QAR Self-Assessment Thinksheet and turn it in with their chart.

Meeting Nelson Mandela

By Rebecca Leon

For use with Step 2: Modeling: title and first 2 paragraphs

"Nelson Mandela is universally known as a humanitarian, an activist, and a freedom fighter," writes 16-year-old Stephanie Chung in her award-winning essay about the famous world leader. "He became a symbol of hope for people suffering injustice all over the world."

Stephanie and 11 other students, grades 6 to 12, recently won an essay contest that took them from their homes in New York City to South Africa, where they got to meet the man they wrote about, Nelson Mandela. The annual competition—sponsored by the Nelson Mandela Foundation—encourages young people around the world to learn about his life and legacy.

Fighting for Equality

For use with Step 3: Guided Practice: "Fighting for Equality" section

Nelson Mandela, who is now in his nineties, led a 30-year struggle to end apartheid (uh-PAR-tiyd), a system of segregation in South Africa that became official government policy in 1948. Under apartheid, the white minority held power over the black majority, who didn't even have the right to vote or leave their homes without an identification card.

Born in the village of Mvezo in 1918, Mandela was the first person in his family to go to school. As a young man, he moved to Johannesburg, the capital of South Africa, to start a career in law. When he arrived, he was deeply affected by the injustices he witnessed. "Mandela started protests, marches, strikes, assemblies, demonstrations, and everything he could to make apartheid leave Johannesburg, disappear from South Africa, and hopefully, depart the world," Khaya Cohen, 12, wrote in her winning essay.

Mandela spent 27 years in prison for trying to change the system; yet he never gave up his unstinting fight for equality. He was even offered his freedom under the condition that he stop fighting apartheid. He refused—and remained in jail. "That was the most valuable lesson I could ever learn," Khaya told *Scope* in an interview.

Changes and Challenges

For use with Step 4: Coaching: "Changes and Challenges" and "An Inspiring Moment" sections

In 1990, Mandela was finally released. He immediately negotiated an end to apartheid. In 1993 he received a Nobel Peace Prize for his efforts. The following year, he was elected President of South Africa, a position he held until 1999.

Today, principles of equality are written into South Africa's constitution, and voting is a right of every citizen. But the country still faces tough challenges, including high unemployment and crime.

An Inspiring Moment

The highlight of the students' trip was the chance to visit Mandela in his office in Johannesburg. They each got to meet with him individually. "He asked me what I wanted to be when I grow up, and he shook my hand," Allen Salama, 12, remembers. "I told him I want to be a doctor, and he was like, 'Good, good.' It made me happy."

Jeniffer Montano said Mandela inspired her to dream big. "Being given the privilege and honor of meeting Mr. Mandela made me realize that if this man had the courage, the determination, and the will to free a nation, then why couldn't simple little me do the same? Why couldn't I give a voice and a face to victims all around the world?" Jeniffer says.

Making Changes Together

For use with Step 5: Independent Application: "Making Changes Together" section

During their trip, the essay winners also teamed up with six South African teens who won the same contest in 2008. (Each year, the contest is held in a different city around the world. In 2008, it was in Johannesburg. In 2009, it was New York City.) Together, the students drafted a Mandela Day charter to encourage teens to apply Mandela's principles to solving problems in the world today. The charter serves as part of international effort to establish Mandela's birthday, July 18, as a day when people around the globe take action to make the world a better place. As Nelson Mandela once said, "For to be free is not merely to cast off one's chains, but to live in a way that respects and enhances the freedom of others."

Reflecting on the whole experience, Allen concluded, "Mandela raised the bar for us, and now we have to reach, or even exceed, his standards. He did his part making a better world, and now we have to follow him and do the same."

Drawing Inferences With Narrative Text

GOAL ● Help students understand how drawing inferences during and after reading can enhance comprehension

I Can Statement

I can draw inferences to enhance my comprehension using the QAR Author & Me Inference Chart.

Reading Cycle and QARs

Reading Cycle: During and After Reading

QAR: *Author & Me:* Using author's clues to identify useful background knowledge and experiences for comprehending narrative text

Materials *(See CD for reproducibles.)*

▶ "The Road Not Taken" by Robert Frost (narrative selection: poem), p. 66 (display copy, one copy for each student)

▶ The Core QARs Poster and QAR and the Reading Cycle Poster (display copy of each)

▶ QAR Author & Me Inference Chart (display copy, one copy for each student)

▶ QAR Self-Assessment Thinksheet (one copy for each student)

BEFORE READING   DURING READING   AFTER READING

Step **1** EXPLICIT EXPLANATION

Begin by explaining the purpose of this lesson as suggested below. (If you have taught Lesson 7 on drawing inferences with informational text, you may want to skip the first paragraph and simply remind students what it means to draw an inference before you speak specifically to the text genre in this lesson.)

The focus of today's lesson is drawing inferences, an important comprehension strategy that active readers use (refer to the QAR and the Reading Cycle Poster) during and after reading. When I draw inferences, I start with the author's clues and call up my own related background knowledge and experiences that will improve my understanding of the text. I use information In My Head to fill in gaps or to enhance the clues provided by the author. The QAR is Author & Me (refer to The Core QARs Poster) because I start with clues from the author, but I build on these clues with In My Head information. When I draw inferences, I'm using information from my head to answer this question: "Building on the author's clues, what background knowledge and experiences do I have that can help me understand the text?"

You're going to see how the QAR Author & Me Inference Chart can help readers make inferences when they read poetry. Most poems are written with just a few words, inviting readers to draw inferences, including making text-to-self connections.

BEFORE READING **DURING READING** AFTER READING

Step **2** MODELING

Display the QAR Author & Me Inference Chart.

Note: If you have not taught Lessons 5 and 6, skip the first sentence below. If your students have participated in those lessons, review the information in the first paragraph. If you have taught Lesson 7, you may wish to skip the entire paragraph, which restates the main ideas from that lesson.

Notice that the QAR Author & Me Inference Chart is similar to the QAR Author & Me Prediction Chart, which you already know how to use. (Note that the similarity in the charts is because predictions are essentially before-reading inferences). *In the Author column, I record the author's clues that are In the Book. In the Me column, I record my own relevant knowledge and experiences. In the Inference column, I write the inference that I create using information from In My Head to expand on the information In the Book.*

Once students have grasped the connections to QAR language, introduce the text.

The title of the poem we are reading today is "The Road Not Taken" by Robert Frost. I can start drawing on knowledge already In My Head because I know something about this poet. I know that Robert Frost lived in New England for most of his life and wrote about his observations of people, relationships, and rural life. For many years, he was the most celebrated poet in America. Even though Frost died in 1963, his works are still very popular today.

As you continue the think aloud, add the underlined words below to the chart.

When I look at the title of this poem, "The Road Not Taken," I visualize myself driving up to an <u>intersection I don't know</u> and deciding to turn down one road instead of another. I'll write <u>The Road Not Taken</u> in the Author column, and my experience with <u>turning down one road instead of another</u> in the Me column. The other road might have been an interesting road to take, but I had to make a choice and I didn't take that road. I can infer that "The Road Not Taken" is about the <u>choices we make in life</u>, and probably about the <u>consequences of those choices</u> too. I'll add those ideas to the Inference column.

QAR Author & Me Inference Chart

AUTHOR	ME	INFERENCE
"The Road Not Taken"	intersection I don't know deciding to turn down one road instead of another	choices we make in life, consequences of those choices

Read aloud the entire poem to the class.

Step **3** GUIDED PRACTICE

Distribute a copy of the poem to each student.

Now that you've heard the whole poem, let's consider just the first two stanzas. We'll look at the author's clues, and then see if we have relevant background knowledge and experiences that lead us to logical inferences. We can also see if we would want to change any of the inferences we've already drawn, now that we have read the whole poem and have more information.

Reread the first two stanzas and underline author's clues that are likely to lead students to call up related background knowledge and experiences.

In the first stanza, Frost says "<u>two roads diverged.</u>" I can write these important clues in the Author column of our chart. When you think about these words, what background knowledge and experiences come to mind?

Call on a few students to elicit their thinking about background knowledge and their own experiences. Ask them how they used the author's words to call up relevant background knowledge and make inferences. If necessary, prompt with specific words and phrases from the first two stanzas. Add the information to the chart as students share; call on some other students to help you fill in the columns.

Sample entries appear in the chart below.

Note: Entering two or three examples into the chart will suffice if students have grasped the strategy. Use more examples only if they will benefit from further guidance.

AUTHOR	ME	INFERENCE
two roads diverge	"diverged" means the two roads go in different directions	It's a symbol for change, or maybe having to leave something or someone.
sorry I could not travel both	Sometimes we want two things, but we can't have them both, and it's hard to choose.	The person in the poem has a big decision to make that will affect his or her life.
long I stood	There are pros and cons to each choice we make.	It's hard for this person to decide which choice will be better in the long run.
having perhaps the better claim	One choice might look a little better than the other.	The person is trying to make a good decision.
had worn them really about the same	The two roads really aren't that different.	Sometimes one choice isn't really better than the other; it's just that the consequences are different.

Note: Seek to move students away from focusing on getting the right answer to thinking in a logical manner. Be sure to praise those who show logical thinking, even if their inferences do not turn out to be accurate.

Step 4 COACHING

Distribute a blank copy of the QAR Author & Me Inference Chart to each student or have them make their own chart on a sheet of notebook paper.

> *Work with a partner to read the third stanza aloud. Take turns reading the different lines. As you're reading, underline any author clues that trigger your background knowledge and experiences and lead you to draw inferences. Enter information into the Author, Me, and Inference columns of your QAR Author & Me Inference Chart.*

Remind students who are experiencing difficulty to ask themselves the following question: "Building on the author's clues, what background knowledge and experiences do I have that can help me understand the text?"

Have pairs form groups of four and share their work. As they pair-share, they should exchange the inferences they drew, explaining why these inferences are logical and useful in interpreting the poem. Afterward, call on a few pairs to share and add information to the class chart. Praise students who show logical thinking.

Sample entries appear below.

AUTHOR	ME	INFERENCE
I kept the first for another day	Sometimes we can choose one thing one time and the other choice at a different time.	This person hopes he/she doesn't have to give up one thing to get the other.
I doubted if I should ever come back	Sometimes choosing one thing makes it impossible to ever go back to the alternative.	The decision this person makes will effect the rest of his/her life.

Step 5 INDEPENDENT APPLICATION

Tell students they will now be working independently.

> *Please reread the fourth stanza. As you read, remember to start with the author's clues, then see if you have any useful background knowledge that can help you draw an inference to further your understanding of the poem. Complete all three columns in your QAR Author & Me Inference Chart. Use author's clues and relevant background knowledge to draw at least two inferences.*

Encourage students who finish early to add more entries to their chart. Invite a few students to add their entries to the class chart. Then call the whole group back together and ask some students to share entries from their charts.

Sample entries for the fourth stanza appear below.

AUTHOR	ME	INFERENCE
Telling this with a sigh ages and ages hence	• sigh = sadness • Some stories are worth telling for generations or to many people.	The speaker regrets leaving the road behind and will share the story of his/her choice and its consequences.
I took the one less traveled by	The poem already said the two roads were about the same	The speaker hopes he/she made a good choice and that there really is an important difference between the two roads.

Step 6 SELF-ASSESSMENT & GOAL-SETTING

Display the I Can Statement and read it aloud.

> *The purpose of this lesson was to help you learn to draw inferences during and after reading to improve your comprehension of this poem. You learned to draw inferences by using the QAR Author & Me Inference Chart. Who can explain how using this chart helps readers draw relevant inferences and comprehend what we read?*

Call on volunteers to share their responses.

> *Now I would like you to think about how you can use the strategy of drawing inferences to help you interpret the meaning of the poem.*

You may want to share with students that Robert Frost said he wrote this poem about his friend Edward Thomas, with whom he walked many times in the woods near London. When they came to different paths, Thomas would choose one but then wonder what they might have missed by not taking the other path. Frost also said about his poem, "You have to be careful of that one. It's a tricky poem—very tricky." Many people think this is an inspirational poem about being self-reliant and independent (taking the road less traveled). But others think that the poet is telling us that we all have to make choices, but we will never know ahead of time what that choice will mean for our lives. Life is about choice, but also about chance.

Conclude the lesson by having students complete a QAR Self-Assessment Thinksheet and turning it in with their individual charts.

The Road Not Taken

By Robert Frost

For use with Step 2: Modeling:
title and entire poem

For use with Step 3: Guided Practice:
first and second stanzas

Two roads diverged in a yellow wood,
And sorry I could not travel both
And be one traveler, long I stood
And looked down one as far as I could
To where it bent in the undergrowth;

Then took the other, as just as fair,
And having perhaps the better claim,
Because it was grassy and wanted wear;
Though as for that the passing there
Had worn them really about the same,

For use with Step 4: Coaching:
third stanza

And both that morning equally lay
In leaves no step had trodden black.
Oh, I kept the first for another day!
Yet knowing how way leads on to way,
I doubted if I should ever come back.

For use with Step 5: Independent Application:
fourth stanza

I shall be telling this with a sigh
Somewhere ages and ages hence:
Two roads diverged in a wood, and I—
I took the one less traveled by,
And that has made all the difference.

Identifying Important Information in Informational Text

GOAL • Help students understand how determining importance based on purposes for reading can enhance comprehension of informational text

I Can Statement

I can determine the important information in the text based on my purposes for reading.

Reading Cycle and QAR

Reading Cycle: Before, During, and After Reading

QAR: *Think & Search:* Using Think & Search Important Information Chart to help guide students as they Think & Search text for important or possibly important information, given their focus questions.

Materials (See CD for reproducibles.)

▶ "We Dared to Lead" by Bryan Brown (informational passage), p. 73 (display copy, one copy for each student)

▶ The Core QARs Poster and QAR and the Reading Cycle Poster (display copy of each)

▶ QAR Think & Search Important Information Chart (display copy and one copy for each pair and each student)

(Save completed charts to use in Lesson 10 on summarizing informational text.)

▶ highlighter

▶ QAR Self-Assessment Thinksheet (one copy for each student)

| BEFORE READING | DURING READING | AFTER READING |

Step 1 EXPLICIT EXPLANATION

Let students know that the purpose of this lesson is to learn the comprehension strategy of identifying important information. To accomplish this, you will be showing them how to use the Think & Search Important Information Chart to organize and remember important text information. Refer to the QAR Reading Cycle poster and remind students that before reading, active readers always have focus questions in mind to help them decide what is important in the text.

Display the QAR Think & Search Important Information Chart.

> *We'll be reading the informational passage "We Dared to Lead." To help us identify the important information in this text, we will be using the QAR Think & Search Important Information Chart to organize information before, during, and after reading. (Refer to The Core QARs Poster). This chart is named after the Think & Search QAR because readers Think & Search the text as they read to find all the important information.*

> *When we read informational text, our purpose is usually to learn something new. (Refer to the QAR and the Reading Cycle Poster.) Before reading, we think about our purpose for reading or what it is we hope to learn. During reading, we keep our purpose in mind because it helps us figure out which information in the text is important to remember. After reading, we use the answers we've found to our questions to help us remember key ideas. We use these ideas for sharing what we've learned when we write summaries or describe the main ideas. As you can see, the Think & Search Important Information Chart can help you during all three parts of the reading cycle.*

Step 2 MODELING

> *Sometimes before-reading questions come from the text, or someone gives them to us—such as when we are reading for a project or an assignment. But many times, as active readers, we create our own focus questions. We look at the title and other features of the text to get some ideas of the content and then think of questions that will help us keep in mind what we're hoping to learn.*

> *The title of this informational passage is "We Dared to Lead." I see that the passage has three headings: "An Unpromising Start," "Three Branches," and "Keep the People Out?" By considering these features—the title and three headings—I can create focus questions to guide me in identifying important information in the text.*

As you think aloud, begin to fill in the QAR Think & Search Important Information Chart.

> *I'll start by thinking about the title. "We Dared to Lead" makes me wonder who "we" refers to, and the word "dared" makes me think there might have been something dangerous about leading. These ideas lead me to my first question: "<u>Who dared to lead, and what made leading dangerous?</u>"*

DURING READING

Display the first section of the text and ask students to follow along as you read it aloud. Remind students that you are especially interested in identifying information to help you answer the question you wrote in the chart. Model reading this section, paragraph by paragraph, and underlining key words and phrases. Here are possibilities for each paragraph:

1. American colonists . . . new country . . . freedom

2. 1781 . . . Continental Congress . . . established federal government . . . Articles of Confederation . . . 13 United States . . . largely independent

3. failure . . . national government . . . little authority

4. 1787 . . . U.S. . . . verge of collapse

5. James Madison . . . other leaders . . . Articles . . . revised . . . Federal Convention

Return to the chart and remind students of the first question, "Who dared to lead and what made leading dangerous?" Do a think-aloud such as the following, entering the notes underlined below in the appropriate columns of the chart.

> *In the Very Important Information column, I'm going to write notes that answer my first question. I learned that <u>James Madison</u> and <u>others were important leaders</u>. What made leadership dangerous was that the <u>U.S.</u> was on the <u>verge of collapse</u>. In the Information That Might Be Important column, I'm going to add <u>Articles of Confederation</u>, <u>national government</u>, <u>little authority</u>, and <u>Federal Convention</u> because these items may help me understand what the leaders were responding to, but they may not be important to explaining why it was dangerous to lead.*

> *Notice that although I read five paragraphs, I boiled things down by focusing on the question, underlining, and then making notes of only the most important information.*

Sample entries for the chart are shown below.

QAR Think & Search Important Information Chart

QUESTION	VERY IMPORTANT INFORMATION	INFORMATION THAT MIGHT BE IMPORTANT, BUT I'M NOT SURE YET
Who dared to lead, and what made leading dangerous?	• James Madison, others: important leaders • U.S., verge of collapse	• Articles of Confederation • national government • little authority • Federal Convention

Step 3 GUIDED PRACTICE

Distribute a copy of the passage to each student.

> *The next section of the text has the heading "An Unpromising Start." Once again, I'm going to think of a question to help focus my reading. I know from the first section that what was starting was a Federal Convention. Turn and talk to a partner and think of a focus question for this part of the text.*

Call on a couple of students to share their ideas and write a focus question on the class chart, such as the following: <u>What made the start of the Federal Convention unpromising?</u>

Note: If students are unfamiliar with vocabulary such as "unpromising," help them understand the meanings of these terms as the words occur in the lesson.

I'm going to read each sentence aloud and then pause briefly. Your job is to underline the important information as we move through the text. Remember that we're especially interested in information that answers our question about the unpromising start.

Read aloud the section, "An Unpromising Start," including the list of participants. Pause for a moment after each sentence to give students a chance to underline. Then ask students to share the underlined information that they believe is definitely important because it is related to the question. Enter this information in the chart. Continue to the next sentence. Sample entries appear below.

QUESTION	VERY IMPORTANT INFORMATION	INFORMATION THAT MIGHT BE IMPORTANT, BUT I'M NOT SURE YET
What made the start of the Federal Convention unpromising?	• Some come late. • Rhode Island not at all • Some delegates don't trust each other.	• Delegates assemble: Philadelphia, May 1781 • Produce radical framework for new government

Step 4 COACHING

Pair students. Distribute a blank copy of the QAR Think & Search Important Information Chart to each pair, or have them draw a copy on a sheet of paper. Ask students to work with partners to read the next section of the passage.

Each pair will share a chart. Ask them to work together to think of a focus question based on the heading of the next section, "Three Branches." They can also take into account the parts of information they have learned so far. Suggest that they take turns reading aloud and underlining.

Circulate around the room to help students who need assistance with formulating a question or with deciding what to underline. Students often have difficulty identifying important information—not an easy task—which results in a tendency to do too much underlining. If you see this happening, remind students to focus on the information related to their question about the three branches.

Bring students together. As pairs share ideas, ask them to explain their thinking. Have students indicate if they agree (and why) or disagree (and why) with the various suggestions. Enter important information in the appropriate column of the class chart as students share. Sample entries appear on the next page.

QUESTION	VERY IMPORTANT INFORMATION	INFORMATION THAT MIGHT BE IMPORTANT, BUT I'M NOT SURE YET
What were the three branches, and what was radical about them?	• legislative, executive, judicial • truly national government • replace Articles of Confederation instead of fixing them • Some worried about too much power over states.	• proposed by Edmund Randolph • 15 resolutions written by Madison, other Virginia and Pennsylvania delegates • Virginia Plan • Gerry and others opposed • delegates accept

Step 5 INDEPENDENT APPLICATION

For independent practice, distribute a blank chart to each student or have everyone create an individual one on a sheet of paper. Tell students to read the remaining section of the text, "Keep the People Out?" Remind them to create a focus question for the section, then underline, and write notes in their chart about the important information, or information that might be important. If there are students who could benefit from continued guidance, bring them together and work with them in a small group.

Call the group together for students to share their work. Encourage them to explain the thinking behind their suggestions for Very Important Information and Information That Might Be Important columns. Have the other students indicate if they agree (and why) or disagree (and why) with the various suggestions. Enter important information and information that might be important in the appropriate column of the class chart. Sample entries appear below.

QUESTION	VERY IMPORTANT INFORMATION	INFORMATION THAT MIGHT BE IMPORTANT, BUT I'M NOT SURE YET
What were the people being kept out of, and who wanted to keep them out?	• one chamber of Congress to be elected by the people • Some delegates don't like this idea, think people lack information to vote properly (Sherman, Gerry).	• Virginia Plan, two chambers of Congress • One chamber should be elected by people (Mason, Madison). • compromise: one chamber elected by popular vote, one chamber appointed by state legislature • 1913 amendment lets voters elect members of Senate.

Step **6** SELF-ASSESSMENT & GOAL SETTING

Display the I Can Statement, read it aloud, and ask students to keep it in mind as they think about what they have learned. Then have them complete a QAR Self-Assessment Thinksheet. When students have completed their self-assessment, ask them to discuss what they learned.

> *Let's talk what you learned about identifying important information before and during reading. How did this help your understanding of the text? In what ways was the QAR Think & Search Important Information Chart helpful? Describe other settings where you can imagine using this kind of chart to help you comprehend the text and remember important information.*

Following this discussion, note that using a chart like this one helps active readers remember and use the information they've identified after reading when they write summaries or main idea statements (see Lessons 10 and 12). Let students know that they will be using the class chart created today for a future lesson on summarizing.

Finally, collect students' work, both the paired and individually completed charts and QAR Self-Assessment Thinksheets.

We Dared to Lead
By Bryan Brown

For use
with Step 2:
Modeling:

title,
introduction

What if you lived under a government that controlled your every move? What if you couldn't attend school, or were persecuted for your religious beliefs? When the American colonists declared independence from Great Britain in 1776, they were determined to create a new country that was dedicated to the freedom of its people.

The task was far from easy. In 1781, the Continental Congress established a federal government under an agreement called the Articles of Confederation. Seeking to avoid a tyrannical central power like the British King, the government's founders allowed the 13 United States to stay largely independent.

Soon, many Americans saw this arrangement as a dismal failure. Under the Articles, the national government had little authority. The country was without an executive to make decisions or enforce laws. Congress, its lawmaking body, lacked crucial powers, such as raising taxes. Deep in debt, the United States couldn't even raise an army.

By 1787, the U.S. was on the verge of collapse. "I am mortified [ashamed] beyond expression when I view the clouds which have spread over [the country]," wrote George Washington, hero of the American Revolution (1775–1783).

James Madison, a member of the Continental Congress from Virginia, and other leaders said that the Articles must be revised. Congress called for a Federal Convention in the spring to do just that.

An Unpromising Start

For use with
Step 3: Guided
Practice:

"An Unpromising
Start"
section

Delegates from the states began to assemble in Philadelphia in May 1787. The gathering at the Pennsylvania State House did not look promising at first. Many delegates were late. Rhode Island had even decided not to participate.

Some of the men didn't trust or like each other. Yet by the end of the long, hot summer, they would produce a document—and the framework for a new government—that was nothing short of radical. Let's listen in on their debate.

Noted Participants

Edmund Randolph, Virginia

Elbridge Gerry, Massachusetts

Roger Sherman, Connecticut

George Mason, Virginia

James Madison, Virginia

William Peterson, New Jersey

Alexander Hamilton, New York

Gunning Bedford, Delaware

Gouverneur Morris, Pennsylvania

Three Branches

For use
with Step 4:
Coaching:

"Three
Branches"
section

Edmund Randolph starts with an unexpected proposal.

Edmund Randolph, Virginia: The Articles of Confederation do not provide for our common defense, security of liberty, or general welfare. Therefore, we propose a truly national government with a legislature, an executive, and a judicial branch.

Some of the delegates are shocked. Instead of fixing the Articles, Randolph wants to replace them! Randolph introduces 15 resolutions written by Madison and other delegates from Virginia and Pennsylvania. The outline for this proposed new government becomes known as the Virginia Plan.

> **Elbridge Gerry, Massachusetts:** Congress sent us here to fix problems with our government! I doubt it would approve of our discussing a system founded on completely different principles.

Despite opposition from Gerry and others, delegates accept a version of the Virginia Plan. But some of them fear that a national government would have too much power over the states.

Keep the People Out?

For use with Step 5: Independent Application:

"Keep the People Out?"

Under the Articles, the legislature of each state chooses its representatives to Congress. But the Virginia Plan calls for two chambers of Congress. One chamber is to be "elected by the people." This sounds like trouble to some of the delegates.

> **Roger Sherman, Connecticut:** The people lack the information to vote properly. They should have as little to do with the government as possible.

> **Gerry:** Exactly.

> **George Mason, Virginia:** You are mistaken. The first chamber of Congress should be the depository [place of safekeeping] of our democratic principles. So it must be elected by the people.

> **James Madison, Virginia:** I agree. Election of one branch of the legislature by the people is a clear principle of free government.

In their final document, the delegates agree on a compromise. The "first chamber" of Congress [the House of Representatives] is to be elected by popular vote. Members of the second chamber [the Senate] are to be appointed by each state legislature. [More than 125 years later, in 1913, the l7th Amendment to the Constitution will allow voters to elect members of the Senate.]

Summarizing Informational Text

GOAL • Help students understand how to create a summary for informational text

I Can Statement

I can write a summary of important ideas in informational text.

Reading Cycle and QAR

Reading Cycle: After Reading

QARs: *Think & Search:* Organizing the important information in the text

Author & Me: Using your own knowledge of how ideas can go together to create a clear and logical representation of the important ideas in the text

Materials *(See CD for reproducibles.)*

▶ "We Dared to Lead" by Bryan Brown (informational passage), p. 73 (display copy, one copy for each student)

▶ The Core QARs Poster and QAR and the Reading Cycle Poster (display copy of each)

▶ QAR Think & Search Important Information Chart (completed class chart and individual students' charts from Lesson 9; also see sample chart on p. 81) (display copy)

▶ QAR Think & Search Summary Web (display copy, one copy for each student)

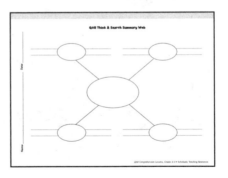

▶ QAR Think & Search Summary Draft (display, one copy for each student)

▶ QAR Self-Assessment Thinksheet (one copy for each student)

Step **1** EXPLICIT EXPLANATION

Explain the purpose of the lesson, referring to The Core QARs Poster and the QARs and the Reading Cycle Poster as appropriate.

> *Today I'm going to teach you about a comprehension strategy called summarizing. Active readers most often summarize after reading to remember what they've read and to share it with others. After I finish reading a text, I often want to be sure that I remember the important information. When readers summarize, they include the important or main ideas the author wants them to understand, without worrying about all the details.*
>
> *When I summarize, I first identify the important information, just as you learned to do in Lesson 9. Then I organize the important information, which is easy to do if I use a web. Finally, I create a summary, which is a new brief text containing the important information. A summary is much shorter than the original text, but it still captures the text's most important information.*
>
> *In Lesson 9, we practiced the first step when we identified the important information in the article "We Dared to Lead." We will create our first summary for that passage using the QAR Think & Search Important Information Chart we completed for that article.*
>
> *The QAR for summarizing is Think & Search. After I search for what is important in the text, I think about how to put the information together to create my brief new text—the summary of the article.*

Step **2** MODELING

Display the following:

- ▶ Completed QAR Think & Search Important Information Chart for "We Dared to Lead" from Lesson 9
- ▶ QAR Think & Search Summary Web
- ▶ QAR Think & Search Summary Draft

Explain to students that you will show them how to use the QAR Think & Search Summary Web to organize the questions and important information in the QAR Think & Search Important Information Chart so they can easily create their new brief text—the summary. Enter the underlined questions below in the chart as you think aloud.

> *Notice that our summary draft has four main parts. First, it has a title or topic. Second, an opening sentence describes what will be in the summary. Third, it contains sentences about each main category. The QAR Think & Search Summary Draft has room for four sentences, but there may be more or fewer sentences depending on the*

amount of information in an article and the number of categories required to include all the important information. Finally, a summary ends with a concluding sentence.

Now I'll start on my summary for "We Dared to Lead." My first step is to make the topic of the summary really clear. Sometimes the title works as the topic, but "We Dared to Lead" could be about people daring to lead in any number of situations. Since the entire passage is about <u>creating the framework of a new government</u>, I am going to use that for the title of my summary. I'll enter that topic in my web. I'm going to write the author's name in parentheses <u>(by Bryan Brown)</u> to remember who wrote the passage.

Next, I am going to decide how many categories of information to include in my summary, using the ideas from my Important Information Chart. I know I had four focus questions, one for each heading in the article. These questions will be the information categories that I will enter into my summary web. For this summary, I will describe four points I learned about how leaders created the framework for the United States government.

Call students' attention to the questions on the QAR Think & Search Important Information Chart and demonstrate how each of those questions can become a category in the summary web. Explain to students that having the topic and categories in mind gives them the information they need for a clear opening sentence to set up the summary.

I have what I need to write my opening sentence. An easy way to create an opening sentence for an informational article is to start with the phrase "This article describes . . . " and then tell the topic and the categories of information in the article. In thinking about the title and the information in this passage, this opening sentence makes sense: <u>This article describes how leaders created the Constitution, a new framework of government for the United States.</u> Since this is just a draft, I can revise my opening sentence later and make it a more interesting lead.

Now I'm ready to go on to the specific ideas that should be included in the summary. The completed QAR Think & Search Important Information Chart for this article will tell me which ideas to select. I'll take notes in my summary web to help me write sentences from my chart so that the summary is in my own words.

Again, I will organize my summary around the four questions in the chart. A good way to start is often by following the order of categories of information in the passage. I'll try that first and decide later if it makes more sense to present the information in another order.

My next step is to decide on the important information from each category that I need to include for a clear, concise summary. For each question, I'll read through the information on the chart that I thought was important. Then I'll write down phrases in the web that will help me remember the idea. I'll use these ideas to write the summary in my own words.

Show students how to use the first question on the chart to create a category on the summary web.

The first question on our chart is "Who dared to lead, and what made leading dangerous?" The beginning of the article gave the names of the leaders and indicated that the country was in a dangerous situation. It was in danger of breaking apart. On *the web, I'm going to name my first category, <u>leaders in a dangerous situation</u>* (enter that information on a line leading to one of the web hub circles).

Model reducing the information in the Very Important Information column of the chart to just the essential points. For each category, enter the phrases that capture the key idea in the smaller ovals on the web.

> *I think the names of the leaders are important, so I'll add <u>James Madison and others</u> to the web. <u>U.S., verge of collapse</u> seems important as well, so I'll add that to the web, too.*
>
> *Now, I'll look at the Information That Might Be Important column to see if there's anything there that should be added to the web. I think it's important to know that the reason the U.S. was on the verge of collapse was that the <u>national government</u> had <u>little authority</u>, so I'll transfer that information to the web.*
>
> *Now I have what I need to write my summary sentence for the first category.*

Demonstrate how to convert the information in the web into one or two sentences you can use in the summary, and write these on the QAR Think & Search Summary Draft. For example: <u>James Madison and others were leaders at a dangerous time because the United States was on the verge of collapse. The problem was caused because the national government had little authority over the states.</u>

Step **3** GUIDED PRACTICE

Point out that you now have your topic, opening sentence, and a sentence for your first category of information for your summary. Tell students that you want them to help you decide on the next category of information associated with the chart question: "What made the start of the Federal Convention unpromising?" (Possible category: Unpromising start for Federal Convention). Enter the phrase you and students agree upon in the second oval in the web.

Read the Very Important Information in the second column of the chart, and ask students to indicate the points they think are the most important and should be entered in the web. Be sure they understand that important information in this case is information that relates directly to the category of an "unpromising start." Enter these important ideas inside the second oval (e.g., <u>some delegates come late; no delegates from Rhode Island; some delegates don't trust each other</u>).

Proceed to the third column in the chart and ask students if any of this information is important enough to enter in the web. Help them see that the information in this column may be useful later but does not relate directly to the category of an unpromising start.

Ask students to turn and talk with a partner to create one or two sentences for the category of "an unpromising start" to add to the summary draft. Remind students that it can be a good idea to use words from the question as the basis for their sentence.

Work with two or three student suggestions and guide the entire group to arrive at a clear sentence (e.g., <u>The start of the Federal Convention was unpromising because some delegates came late, Rhode Island didn't send anyone at all, and the delegates didn't trust one another.</u>) Add this sentence to the class summary draft.

Step 4 COACHING

Distribute a copy of a summary web and a summary draft to each student. For the next step, students will continue to work with their partner.

> *You and your partner are going to work on the next section of the summary web and summary draft together. Begin by looking at the third question on our chart. Decide on a good category for this question and write the category on an oval on the web. Transfer the most important information for this category from our chart to the web. Then use your notes on the web to create a sentence to add to the summary draft.*

When students have finished, ask two pairs to form a square of four students and share their sentences. Ask them to compare and contrast each of their examples and what they can learn from seeing each other's sentences. Have a few pairs share their sentences, then add a suitable sentence for this category to the class summary draft (e.g., <u>The three branches were the different parts of the new government: legislative, executive, and judicial. Some thought this was a radical idea because it gave the federal government so much power over the states.</u>)

Step 5 INDEPENDENT APPLICATION

Distribute students' individual Important Information Charts from Lesson 9, or direct their attention to the completed class chart that is on display.

> *You'll be working independently using your chart from Lesson 9 to complete your summary web and your summary draft. Think of a category for the fourth question. Then, on the web, enter the important information from the chart that you want to use in your summary. Use the notes on your web to capture the important information and create the next sentence for your summary draft.*

Remind students who are experiencing difficulty in being selective to focus on the information that answers the question on the chart: "What were the people being kept out of, and who wanted to keep them out?" Guide those students who are having trouble with wording a sentence to use words from the question as their starting point (e.g., <u>The people were being kept out of electing the Congress by people who thought they lacked the information to vote properly.</u>).

Tell students who finish early to try their hand at drafting a closing sentence for the summary that indicates what they learned from the passage.

Bring the group back together. Call on two or three students to share the information they entered in their web and the sentence they composed for the fourth category. Enter a suitable sentence in the class summary draft.

Inform students that summaries usually end with a closing sentence telling what the reader learned from reading the passage. Have them turn and talk to their partner about a possible closing sentence. Ask two or three students to share, and enter a suitable closing sentence in the class summary draft (e.g., <u>This article shows that leaders faced many challenges in creating a new government for the United States.</u>)

Step 6 SELF-ASSESSMENT & GOAL SETTING

Have students discuss what they learned about creating a summary. Be sure they understand that creating a summary requires the following three steps:

1. Identifying the important information, which they accomplished with the QAR Think & Search Important Information Chart

2. Organizing the important information, which they accomplished with the summary web

3. Writing a brief new text containing the important information, which they accomplished with the summary draft

Display the I Can Statement and ask students to keep it in mind as they think about what they have learned. Finally, have students complete the QAR Self-Assessment Thinksheet and turn it in with their completed summary web and summary draft.

Note: This lesson shows students how to create a draft of a summary. You can build on this foundation by having them revise their draft to create a more polished summary. For example, you can guide students to write an interesting lead and strong concluding sentence and have them decide where information such as the date and location of the Federal Convention should be included.

Summarizing is a complex process that can prove challenging for many students. The more opportunities they have to practice summarizing, the better. Have students practice using their tools for summarizing in a range of disciplinary contexts. Social studies and science texts provide excellent opportunities for extended practice in summarizing important information.

QAR Think & Search Important Information Chart

(Sample for Lesson 9)

Note: All the think-alouds in this lesson use the information presented in this chart. There may be slight variations between this chart and the one your class produced in Lesson 9, so use your judgment about whether to use it as is, or create a version that includes additional important information that your class discussed.

QUESTION	VERY IMPORTANT INFORMATION	INFORMATION THAT MIGHT BE IMPORTANT, BUT I'M NOT SURE YET
Who dared to lead, and what made leading so dangerous?	• James Madison, others: important leaders • U.S., verge of collapse	• Articles of Confederation • national government • little authority • Federal Convention
What made the start of the Federal Convention unpromising?	• Some come late. • Rhode Island not at all • Some delegates don't trust each other.	• delegates assemble: Philadelphia, May 1781 • produce radical framework for new government
What were the three branches, and what was radical about them?	• legislative, executive, judicial • truly national government • replace Articles of Confederation instead of fixing them • Some worried about too much power over states.	• proposed by Edmund Randolph • 15 resolutions written by Madison, other Virginia and Pennsylvania delegates • Virginia Plan • Gerry and others opposed • delegates accept
What were the people being kept out of, and who wanted to keep them out?	• one chamber of Congress to be elected by the people • Some delegates don't like this idea, think people lack information to vote properly (Sherman, Gerry).	• Virginia Plan, two chambers of Congress • One chamber should be elected by people (Mason, Madison). • compromise: one chamber elected by popular vote, one chamber appointed by state legislature • 1913 amendment lets voters elect members of Senate.

Identifying Important Information in Narrative Text

GOAL ● Help students understand how determining importance based on purposes for reading can enhance comprehension of narrative text

I Can Statement

I can determine the important information in the text based on my purposes for reading.

Reading Cycle and QAR

Reading Cycle: Before, During, and After Reading

QAR: *Think & Search:* Close reading for author clues related to focus questions

Materials *(See CD for reproducibles.)*

▶ "The Case of the Squished Tomatoes: A Courtroom Mystery" by Marvin Miller (narrative passage), p. 88 (display copy, one copy for students) (2 files on CD)

▶ The Core QARs Poster and QAR and the Reading Cycle Poster (display copy of each)

▶ QAR Think & Search Important Information Chart (display copy, one copy for each student)

▶ QAR Self-Assessment Thinksheet (one copy for each student)

BEFORE READING   DURING READING   AFTER READING

Step 1 EXPLICIT EXPLANATION

Note: If you have led students through Lesson 9 on identifying important information in informational text, establish the connection and review what they have learned.

Explain to students that the purpose of this lesson is to learn to identify important information in stories, using their knowledge of story elements and the QAR Think & Search Important Information Chart.

Today I will be teaching you how to use the QAR Think & Search Important Information Chart to identify important information when reading stories or narratives. We'll be reading the passage "The Case of the Squished Tomatoes: A Courtroom Mystery". and identifying the information in it.

Display the Core QARs Poster, the QAR and the Reading Cycle Poster, and the QAR Think & Search Important Information Chart. Refer to the displays as indicated in the think-aloud below.

You can use the Think & Search Important Information Chart to record information before, during, and after reading narrative text. Before reading, we activate what we know about the type of story we will be reading and the kind of information it is likely to contain. Knowing that we'll be reading a mystery today already gives me some ideas about what to expect in the text. During reading, we keep in mind what we are learning about the various story elements, such as the characters and setting. After reading, we'll use information from our chart to address our questions.

We may find some important details Right There in one place in the text, but readers usually need to Think & Search across the text to find all the information necessary to answer the questions. Since authors create stories using elements such as character, setting, problem, and solution, we can use what we know about these elements to figure out what is important.

Today's story is a mystery. The characters' actions are very important, and reading closely for details about them will help us solve the mystery. The QAR Think & Search Important Information Chart will guide our note-taking and help us remember details about the characters as we try to solve the mystery.

DURING READING

Step **2** MODELING

Invite students to share what they know about the mystery that would help them determine important text information in this genre (e.g., a detective type of character, a mystery to be solved, things are not always what they seem).

Lead students to understand that the main questions we have when we read this genre focus on the nature of the mystery and sorting out relevant, or important, clues from distracting information that the author is using to keep us guessing. Enter the underlined questions below in the first column of the chart as you think aloud.

Since I know this is a mystery, my first important question asks <u>what the mystery actually is</u>. I'll enter this as my first question in the QAR Think & Search Important Information Chart. I'll write a second question to remind me to pay attention to the <u>clues</u> the author gives me, and to think about which ones are the most important. And my third question, <u>Where does this mystery take place</u>?, helps me attend to information about the setting that may be important. As I read, I'll pause and write an exclamation point for information I think is very important and a question mark for information I think might possibly be important.

QAR Think & Search Important Information Chart

QUESTION	VERY IMPORTANT INFORMATION	INFORMATION THAT MIGHT BE IMPORTANT, BUT I'M NOT SURE YET
What is the mystery?		
What clues can help me solve the mystery?		
Where does this mystery take place?		

Then display the title and first section of the passage, so students can follow along as you code the text for importance.

I'm going to code the important information as I read the passage. The title, "The Case of the Squished Tomatoes: A Courtroom Mystery," suggests that a crime was committed. I'll put an exclamation point next to the word "Case" because I've heard it used on TV crime dramas. I'm going to mark "Courtroom" with a question mark because it may the setting where the mystery takes place or just where the trial is being held. I'm marking "Squished Tomatoes" with a question mark because I'm not sure how a squished tomato will be part of the story, but the title says that's what the case is about. This is all information that I can enter in the Very Important and the Might Be Important categories of the chart.

As I continue reading, I'm going to think of other story elements besides setting. I'm wondering who the main characters are, so I'm adding that question to my chart.

Sample entries for the chart appear below.

QUESTION	VERY IMPORTANT INFORMATION (!)	INFORMATION THAT MIGHT BE IMPORTANT, BUT I'M NOT SURE YET (?)
What is the mystery?	• Case of . . .	• squished tomatoes
What clues can help me solve the mystery?		
Where does this mystery take place?		• courtroom
Who are the important characters?		

Read the first section of the mystery, and code important ideas as you read and refer to the questions on the chart. Think-aloud comments may include the following:

?: "Thief will go to prison for a long time" might be important information because whoever is caught may claim to be innocent.

!: Andrew Turner is likely to be important—he's been accused.

? $2000.00 was stolen from Hopp-n-Shop (!), so the mystery is who the thief is and how they will catch him, but the amount may not be important.

!: Harvey Hopp is likely to be an important character—he was the one who was robbed and has information as a witness.

?: "Hopp left at 9:15, and the alarm went off at 9:56" might be important since that's when the burglary happened.

?: The exhibit that shows the police report says Car #6 was dispatched, and I know that sometimes it matters which policeman is the one at the scene, but a lot of times it doesn't. So I'll need to wait and see about that.

Enter the coded information into the chart, as illustrated below.

QUESTION	VERY IMPORTANT INFORMATION (!)	INFORMATION THAT MIGHT BE IMPORTANT, BUT I'M NOT SURE YET (?)
What is the mystery?	• Case of . . . • $2000.00 was stolen from the Hopp-n-Shop.	• squished tomatoes
What clues can help me solve the mystery?		• police car 6 • burglar alarm at 9:56 pm
Where does this mystery take place?	• Hopp-n-Shop Grocery Store	• courtroom
Who are the important characters?	• Andrew Turner, employee of Hopp-n-Shop, accused of stealing. • Harvey Hopp, owner of Hopp-n-Shop, first witness	• Andrew claims innocence. • Harvey locked store at 9:15 pm.
What is the solution to the mystery?		

Step 3 GUIDED PRACTICE

Distribute a copy of the passage to each student, but <u>do not give them the verdict (which is in a separate file on the CD)</u>.

> *Now you'll practice identifying important information from our mystery. Follow along as I read the next section, and code the text as you've just seen me do. Use an exclamation point next to information that you think is very important and a question mark next to information that you think might be important. Your coding will help us decide what to add to our chart.*

Read the next section aloud, pausing after each phrase or sentence to give students a chance to code the text. Then ask them to share any new important information (e.g., <u>safe open, money gone; someone could have seen Harvey open the safe and remembered the combination; door of the store unlocked; writing from tomato juice on inside of store window; tomatoes damaged and half-eaten</u>). Have students come up and add their new information to the class chart and explain why they think it is or might be important.

Step 4 COACHING

Distribute a copy of the QAR Think & Search Important Information Chart to each student or have them draw a chart on a sheet of paper. Allow time for students to copy the questions in the first column of the class chart onto their individual charts. Tell them they need not enter the information in the other columns at this time.

Ask partners to take turns reading the next section of the passage and remind them to pay attention to the illustration of Exhibit A. After partners have finished reading, they should discuss the text and illustration and then code the important information in each using exclamation points and question marks. Each partner then enters the coded information into the appropriate column in their individual chart. Remind them to use notes rather than complete sentences. As students work, circulate around the room, offering assistance as needed. Identify partners who are doing an especially good job with the task.

When students have finished this task, call on the pairs you identified to share what they think should be added to the class chart, based on their coding. This information could include the following:

What clues can help me solve the mystery?

1. worker hid in the store before closing, came out of hiding when alone in the store
2. half-eaten sandwich with unusual teeth marks
3. Andrew Turner's teeth marks matched those in the cheese
4. list of sandwich ingredients

Students' choices of what information is very important or may be important will vary, so be sure to ask them to explain the logic underlying their choices.

Step 5 INDEPENDENT APPLICATION

Tell students that it is time for them to practice coding important information in the rest of the mystery on their own. Remind them to add information they think is important, marked with an exclamation point, to the second column, and to add information that might be important, coded with a question mark, in the third column. Then they should add this final question to their chart: <u>What is the solution to the mystery?</u> Tell them to write their opinion about whether Andrew is innocent or guilty and to use the information from their chart to justify their opinion.

Information added to the chart from this section could include the following but will vary in where students place the information:

1. Andrew information: loved to eat, allergic to tomatoes
2. Clues: Andrew snuck into Hopp's office to eat sandwich; girlfriend did not know the time of the call with Andrew.

Circulate around the room, offering assistance and looking for students who are doing an especially good job with the task. Then ask these students to share their answers to the question of how the mystery got solved. Call on students to identify the three clues the jury considered when determining Andrew's guilt. (He worked for the Hopp-n-Shop and hid in the closet; he lied about his tomato allergy; his teeth matched the sandwich bite marks.)

Then display "The Verdict" or read it aloud. Ask students to compare their opinions and the list of what they thought was important information to the actual solution to the question of who robbed Hopp-n-Shop.

BEFORE READING   DURING READING   **AFTER READING**

Step 6 SELF-ASSESSMENT & GOAL-SETTING

Lead students in a brief discussion of what they learned about identifying important information in a mystery or other narrative texts.

> *How did coding and the QAR Think & Search Important Information Chart help you understand the text and pay attention to the most important clues? Describe other opportunities to use coding and the chart to help you find and remember important ideas.*

Tell students that they will be returning to the chart for a future lesson on summarizing a story.

Display the I Can Statement and ask students to keep it in mind as they think about what they have learned. Have them complete their QAR Self-Assessment Thinksheet. Collect their charts for evaluation and be sure to save these charts for use in Lesson 12. Also collect their QAR Self-Assessment Thinksheets.

For use with Step 2: Modeling:

title and first 8 paragraphs

The Case of the Squished Tomatoes: A Courtroom Mystery

By Marvin Miller

Court is about to begin and you are the jury. Read carefully, take notes, and look at the evidence. Do whatever you can to discover the truth.

Ladies and gentlemen of the jury:

If a burglary takes place and a great deal of money is stolen, the thief may be sent to prison for a very long time.

Carefully consider this serious penalty as you listen to the evidence presented here today.

Andrew Turner is accused of stealing $2,000 from the safe of the Hopp-n-Shop Grocery Store. Andrew Turner, who worked at Hopp-n-Shop, says he is innocent.

Harvey Hopp is the first witness in this case. Here is Hopp's testimony:

"My name is Harvey Hopp. I own the Hopp-n-Shop Grocery Store. On the evening of June 5, around 9:15 p.m., I locked up the store for the night and headed home. I learned later that at 9:56 p.m., the burglar alarm for the store's safe went off. Luckily, the police came right away."

EXHIBIT A is an official record of the burglar alarm report.

D.D. 8

| Police Department Burglar Alarm Report | PRECINCT 18th |
| | REPORT NUMBER 842A |

DATE
June 5, 2010

TIME
9:56 pm

LOCATION:
Hopp-n-Shopp Grocery Store
82 Prospect St.

Police car #6 dispatched.

EXHIBIT A

STOP

For use with Step 3: Guided Practice:

next 8 paragraphs

When the police arrived, they found that the door of the store was unlocked. In searching the store, they found the office safe open. The money inside had been stolen. In a corner of the store, near a vegetable bin, police found a basket of spilled tomatoes. The thief had left his or her mark. Damaged tomatoes, some half eaten, were on the floor. On the window, with the juice of a squished tomato, the thief had written the word "DELICIOUS!"

EXHIBIT B is a photograph of the damage done by the thief.

The state questioned Harvey Hopp further. First the question, and then his answer:

Q: Are you sure you locked the door to the store on the evening of the burglary?

A: I'm certain.

Q: Did anyone have the combination to your safe?

A: I'm the only one. But it's possible that someone who worked for me could have seen me open the safe and remembered the combination.

Q: Does anyone else use your office?

A: No. I'm the only one. But sometimes my workers come in if they want to speak with me privately.

DELICIOUS!

TOMATOES 63¢

EXHIBIT B

STOP

For use with Step 4: Coaching:

next 4 paragraphs

Since there was no evidence that the door was broken into, police reasoned the burglary was an inside job. They believed that one of Hopp's workers hid in the store before closing. Then, when Hopp locked the store for the night, the thief came out of hiding and was alone in the store.

Inside the office wastebasket, near the safe, police found a half-eaten sandwich. The sandwich was sent to the crime lab for examination. A slice of cheese from the sandwich showed important evidence. There were unusual teeth marks on the cheese. The bite marks showed that the person eating the sandwich had a front tooth missing.

EXHIBIT C is the police lab report.

The teeth marks from the cheese were compared with the teeth of the people who worked in the store. Andrew Turner's teeth marks matched exactly! His front tooth is missing, and all other teeth matched the marks on the cheese. On this basis, Andrew Turner was arrested and is on trial here today.

EVIDENCE Sandwich	POLICE DEPARTMENT LABORATORY REPORT	REFERENCE Hopp-n-Shopp Grocery Store 82 Prospect St.
DATE RECEIVED June 5, 2010 DATE ANALYZED June 6, 2010		

Report on partial sandwich found in wastebasket

CONTENTS OF SANDWICH
Sandwich contained cheese, ham, onions, hot green peppers, cucumbers on white bread. Thick layer of catsup on upper slice of bread.

DESCRIPTION OF BITE MARKS
Teeth marks in cheese reveal the following: Upper left central incisor missing (#9). Malocclusion of upper left first bicuspid (#13). Other teeth of normal size.

Harry Whitcomb, PhD.
LABORATORY DIRECTOR

EXHIBIT C

For use with Step 5: Independent Application:

next 11 paragraphs and final section, The Verdict

Turner had worked for Mr. Hopp for seven months. But recently there was trouble between them. It seemed that Turner loved to eat. He nibbled on store food without paying for it.

The court asked Andrew Turner about this:

"Food? Sure I love food. Anyone can see that. Just look at the size of my stomach. I love to nibble.

"But I hate tomatoes. I'm allergic to them. Every time I eat a tomato my eyes get watery and I break out in a rash."

Turner was asked about the half-eaten sandwich in the wastebasket. He said the following:

"I admit it. That's the sandwich I ate. But I didn't eat it the night of the burglary. I got hungry in the afternoon. I know Mr. Hopp doesn't like me eating. So I sneaked into his office while he was in the front of the store and ate that fantastic sandwich. When I saw Hopp coming, I tossed the last of it in the wastebasket."

Andrew Turner's lawyer says that at the time the store alarm rang, Andrew was at home talking on the telephone with his girlfriend, Nancy King.

Miss King said that they did talk on the phone for about a half hour. However, she was not sure of the exact time of the call.

Andrew Turner's lawyer says that Nancy King provides Turner with an alibi. And since Turner is allergic to tomatoes, he must be innocent.

Ladies and gentlemen of the jury:

You have just heard the "Case of the Squished Tomatoes." You must now make a decision. Be sure to look carefully at the evidence in EXHIBITS A, B, and C. Did Andrew Turner steal the money from Hopp-n-Shopp's safe? Or is he innocent?

The Verdict

Andrew Turner broke into the safe. Turner said that he couldn't be the burglar because he was allergic to tomatoes. In EXHIBIT C, the lab report describes the sandwich Turner was eating. It was topped with catsup.

Turner admitted it was his sandwich, but forgot that catsup is made from tomatoes. Andrew Turner wasn't really allergic to tomatoes.

It was Turner who opened the safe and wrote the sign on the window.

Summarizing Narrative Text

GOAL • Help students understand how to create a summary for a narrative text

I Can Statement

I can write a summary of important ideas in narrative text.

Reading Cycle and QARs

Reading Cycle: After Reading

QARs: *Think & Search:* Organizing the important information in the text

Author & Me: Using your own knowledge of how ideas can go together to create a clear and logical representation of the important ideas in the text

Materials *(See CD for reproducibles.)*

▶ "The Case of the Squished Tomatoes: A Courtroom Mystery" by Marvin Miller (narrative passage), p. 88 (display copy, one copy for each student) (Use passage on CD without step notations.)

▶ The Core QARs Poster and QAR and the Reading Cycle Poster (display copy of each)

▶ QAR Think & Search Important Information Chart (completed class chart from Lesson 11) (also see sample chart on p. 85) (display copy, one copy for each student)

▶ QAR Think & Search Summary Web (display copy, one copy for each student)

▶ QAR Think & Search Summary Draft (display copy, one copy for each student)

▶ QAR Self-Assessment Thinksheet (one copy for each student)

BEFORE READING   DURING READING   AFTER READING

Step 1 EXPLICIT EXPLANATION

When you explain the focus of this lesson, include the first sentence below only if you've taught Lesson 10 on summarizing of informational text.

Display the posters. Refer to them as you think aloud.

You've already learned to summarize informational text, and today you will be learning to summarize a story or a narrative. Summarizing is an important comprehension strategy used after reading (refer to the QAR and the Reading Cycle

Poster). When readers summarize, they include the most important ideas the author wants them to understand, without worrying about all the details. The QARs most useful for creating a summary are Think & Search, since you are putting ideas together from throughout the passage, and Author & Me, since you must also use information from your head to organize the text information in a way that makes sense (refer to The Core QARs Poster).

I will be teaching you how to summarize a story by returning to the narrative we read in Lesson 11, "The Case of the Squished Tomatoes: A Courtroom Mystery." When readers summarize, they must first identify the important information. We completed this step when we filled in our QAR Think & Search Important Information Chart for this story, so we will use this chart as the basis for our summary.

After identifying the important information, the other two steps in summarizing a narrative are to organize the important information (Think & Search) and then to create a brief new text—the summary of the story.

Note: You may want to highlight the extra step in summarizing a narrative text, in contrast to informational text. Informational text summaries generally follow the flow of the passage. Narrative summaries often draw on information throughout the text, requiring the additional step of organizing the important information in a logical way (e.g., using the story elements).

DURING READING

Step **2** MODELING

Display the following:

▶ QAR Think & Search Summary Web

▶ QAR Think & Search Summary Draft

▶ completed QAR Think & Search Important Information Chart for "The Case of the Squished Tomatoes: A Courtroom Mystery" from Lesson 11

If students participated in Lesson 10, remind them that these are the same graphic organizers they used to summarize informational text. Explain that you will show them how to use the QAR Think & Search Summary Web to organize important information in the story. The web will help you organize the questions and important information in the chart into categories so you can organize ideas for the summary. Then you will show them how to use the information in the web to start writing sentences on the QAR Think & Search Summary Draft. This will be their brief new text—the summary. Think aloud as you write the underlined material below in the web and summary draft.

In the center of the QAR Think & Search Summary Web, I'll enter the title and author, "The Case of the Squished Tomatoes: A Courtroom Mystery" by Marvin Miller, since that is the focus of this summary. I'll start my actual summary using the QAR Think & Search Summary Draft. Since the title has enough information in it to tell my reader what I am summarizing, I can just use the title of the story as the title of my summary. Below the title, I'm going to include an introductory sentence—a sentence that describes what this summary is about. An easy way to create an introductory sentence for a story summary is to start with "This story is about . . ." I'll write: This story is about a courtroom case involving a grocery store burglary. This is a draft, and I can revise this introductory sentence later to create an interesting lead.

Return to the summary web. Explain the four story elements that are the core of the complete summary of a narrative text—characters, setting, problem, and solution—and use one to label each of four outer circles in the web.

A good story summary, like a good summary of informational text, provides important information and omits the less important details. It fits our expectations that stories have predictable elements, such as characters, setting, problem, and solution. We can organize our story summary around these elements by putting one in each of the circles on our web to organize the ideas from our Important Information Chart.

Notice how I created my categories representing story elements, which are found throughout the chart. I started my web with the story elements of setting and main characters, rather than with the problem and solution. I did this because I need to explain the setting and the characters in my summary before I can explain the conflict or problem and how it was solved.

Referring to the chart, add information about the setting (e.g., courtroom for trial; grocery store for robbery) to the summary web. Then model how you write a sentence about the setting to add to the summary draft.

Now that I have information about the setting in the first circle in my summary web, I can take that information and turn it into a sentence for my summary draft. Let me see, I think I'll write: The story takes place in a courtroom where someone is on trial for robbing a grocery store.

Step **3** GUIDED PRACTICE

Point out that you now have two sentences for your summary: the introductory sentence and a sentence about the setting. Explain to students that you would like them to help you create the next sentence. Call their attention to the circle in the web for main characters.

Let's think together about the next category of information in our summary web—the main characters. Take a look at what we wrote about the characters in the class chart and tell me what you think we should enter in our web.

Have students suggest information about the main characters that should be put in the summary web. Possible responses might include the following: Andrew Turner, employee at Hopp-n-Shop; Harvey Hopp, owner of Hopp-n-Shop.

Write this information on the web. Then turn students' attention to the summary draft. Ask them to turn to a partner and discuss a sentence about the main characters that can be added to the summary draft. Have a few students share their sentences. Then write a sentence or two that the group agrees captures key information about the main characters (e.g., There are two important characters in this story. Andrew Turner is an employee at Hopp-n-Shop accused of stealing, and Harvey Hopp is the owner of the grocery store that was robbed).

Step **4** COACHING

Pass out a copy of a summary web and a summary draft to each student. Have students add information to their individual charts so that it matches the one you are modeling, explaining that they will need this when they work independently later in the lesson. For this step, have partners work together.

> *You and your partner will complete the next category in the summary web, the story's problem. Use ideas about the problem in the chart. Enter the key ideas in your own summary web. Then work with your partner to create a sentence about the problem. Add your sentence to your individual summary draft.*

Monitor the progress of pairs, and be sure to provide coaching as needed. Students may try to transfer too much information to their summary web. If this happens, have partners select just two or three ideas to transfer. If students have difficulty composing a summary sentence, suggest that they start with the words "The problem in this story was . . ." (e.g., The problem in this story was the Hopp-n-Shop robbery and Andrew's claim that he is innocent). When pairs have completed their summary sentence, ask them to form squares of four students. Ask the squares to compare the information about the problem in their summary webs, as well as the sentences they added to their summary drafts.

Reconvene the group and ask two or three squares to share similarities and differences they observed when comparing their summary webs and summary drafts.

Step **5** INDEPENDENT APPLICATION

Students will work independently to summarize the important information from the last category in the web—the solution.

> *For this step, I want you to work independently to complete your summary web and summary draft as you focus on the last category, the solution. Review ideas about the solution in the Important Information Chart, and enter the important information about the solution in your summary web. Use an entry from your web to create a sentence describing the solution to add to your summary draft.*

Monitor students and provide assistance as needed. When students are working with their webs, make sure that they are being selective about the information they enter. Provide assistance to students who may have difficulty with wording the sentence, suggesting that they begin with the words "The problem was solved when . . ."

Then call the group back together. Ask several students to share the information they entered in their summary web and the sentence they composed for their summary draft. A possible sentence about the solution might include the following: <u>The problem was solved when the lab report found catsup on the sandwich Andrew admitted he ate on the day of the burglary.</u> Guide students to the understanding that in a summary, it is not necessary to present details about all of the clues. Also point out that in summarizing a narrative, a closing sentence may not be needed, since the final sentence of the summary explains the overall point of the story—in this case, the solution to the problem or mystery.

Step **6** SELF-ASSESSMENT & GOAL-SETTING

Have students discuss what they learned about summarizing narrative texts in this lesson. Explain that summarizing a story or narrative requires the same three steps as summarizing an informational text: (1) identifying the important information, which can be accomplished by using an Important Information Chart, (2) organizing the important information, which can be accomplished by using a summary web, and (3) writing a brief new text containing the important information, which can be accomplished by using a summary draft.

You may wish to provide students with the opportunity to practice using the summary for an authentic purpose. For example, they may "review" the story for a class newspaper or create a summary that would entice someone to read the passage. Point out the importance of interesting leads for drawing the reader into the summary and determining what details to include without giving away the resolution. Allow students time to complete the second draft of their summaries. If time allows, you may ask a few students to share their second drafts.

Display the I Can Statement and ask students to keep it in mind as they think about what they have learned.

> *Think about how you could use summarizing in other areas and how you can add this strategy to your personal toolkit for reading. Please complete your QAR Self-Assessment Thinksheet and turn it in with your completed assignments (i.e., summary web, summary draft, final version if completed).*

Summarizing is a valuable yet challenging strategy for many students. Reinforce summarizing skills with narrative texts during language arts instruction for authentic purposes, such as student book talks or book sales, to encourage others to read a favorite book, for reading log entries in a multiple text unit, and in social studies when reading informational storybooks or informational texts using narrative structures (e.g., textbook sections using narrative to describe historical events).

Questioning With Informational Text

GOAL

● Help students understand how to generate and respond to questions appropriate to each phase of the reading cycle

I Can Statement

I can generate and answer appropriate questions before, during, and after reading.

Reading Cycle and QAR

Reading Cycle: Before, During, and After Reading

QARs: *Right There:* Identifying important information
Think & Search: Connecting ideas across text
Author & Me: Making text-to-self connections
On My Own: Brainstorming prior to reading

Materials *(See CD for reproducibles.)*

▶ "Protected Paradise" by Cody Crane (informational passage), p. 102 (display copy, one copy for each student)

▶ The Core QARs Poster and QAR and the Reading Cycle Poster (display copy of each)

▶ QAR Reading Cycle Chart (one copy for each student)

▶ QAR Self-Assessment Thinksheet (one copy for each student)

BEFORE READING   DURING READING   AFTER READING

Step 1 EXPLICIT EXPLANATION

Tell students that questioning in school often means answering questions that teachers ask or that occur in textbooks and on tests. However, readers can learn as much, if not more, by creating their own questions while reading.

Today we'll be focusing on learning to ask—not just answer—appropriate questions before, during, and after reading an informational text. Our work with

questioning will connect with what you've already learned about the reading cycle. Active readers improve their comprehension by using questions strategically throughout the reading cycle.

Step **2** MODELING

Display the QAR Reading Cycle Chart.

Note: We recommend teaching Lesson 4 before this lesson. Then you can begin by reminding students to think about what they have learned about QARs and the reading cycle.

Tell students that you will be using the QAR Reading Cycle Chart to help you keep track of three things: (1) the questions you have created for each phase of the reading cycle, (2) the QAR you think will be most helpful in answering the question, and (3) the information you think will contribute to a good answer for the question.

Display the QAR and the Reading Cycle Poster. Remind students that when we ask questions to support our comprehension, we use different QARs during each phase of the reading cycle. Elicit the three phases from students: before reading, during reading, and after reading. Have them explain why each QAR identified in the poster is appropriate to that particular phase of the reading cycle. Guide them to recall the connection between the QARs and the reading cycle: generating background knowledge and prediction before reading (On My Own/Author & Me), using text information and making connections during reading (Right There, Think & Search, Author & Me), and reflecting on their connections to the text and the influence of the text on their thinking after reading (Author & Me). You could use words to this effect:

> *Active readers create questions that help them think more deeply about what they are reading. We've learned that before reading a new text or text section, questions help us brainstorm what we know that could help us understand the text and make predictions about information it is likely to present. During reading, questions help us identify important text information. After reading, questions can help us review and summarize important ideas and make connections, especially text-to-self and text-to-world connections. In short, questions support our understanding throughout the reading cycle.*
>
> *Before reading, active readers think about the title and the kind of text they are about to read to gain a sense of what to expect from the text and how to approach it. The passage we're reading today, "Protected Paradise," is an informational text, so I know that I'll probably be learning facts and ideas about a topic.*
>
> *I'll think On My Own about the words in the title, "Protected Paradise." I know the word "paradise" is used to describe a beautiful and special place. Does "protected" mean that the paradise is already protected or that it needs protection? That's an Author & Me QAR, because I'll need information from the author to answer it.*
>
> *I'm going to use the QAR Reading Cycle Chart to organize my questions and keep track of my answers.*

In the Before-Reading Questions section of the chart, enter the QAR and question, as shown below.

QAR Reading Cycle Chart

QAR	MY QUESTIONS	MY ANSWERS
	BEFORE-READING QUESTIONS	
Author & Me	paradise already protected or needs protecting?	

Note: Before reading, On My Own QARs occur when students are brainstorming based on minimal information about the text: title, opening illustration, author's name, and genre. When students shift from brainstorming to prediction before reading, by definition, the QAR shifts from On My Own (my opinion about the possibilities) to Author & Me (my predictions based on author information).

DURING READING

Now I'll read the first two paragraphs and see if I can find an answer to my question.

After reading, as you think aloud, enter the underlined words below in the My Answers column of the chart.

I learned that the paradise, which is a large section of the Pacific Ocean, <u>has now been protected</u>. Former President George W. Bush created <u>three new marine monuments</u>, which will help <u>conserve the ocean</u>.

Note: This lesson models note-taking to save time, but you can write the full question and answer if your students need to see that modeled.

Step 3 GUIDED PRACTICE

Have students help you generate questions to guide the reading of the next section of text. Ask them to consider the text information they have gathered so far, as well as the heading of the next section, "Hot Spot." Refer to the QAR and the Reading Cycle Poster and remind students that during reading, questions are usually Author & Me, Think & Search, and Right There.

Based on what we know about the article so far, think about the kinds of questions that it would be helpful to ask next.

Model by suggesting one or two questions, then elicit questions from students, discussing the QARs that each question represents, then adding each one to the chart under the During-Reading Questions section.

Note: Enter *only* the questions in the QAR Reading Cycle Chart. The QAR to use in answering each question will not become visible until *during reading*. The QAR is determined as you read with the question in mind, and the answer is entered following reading.

Questions and QARs for the "Hot Spot" section might include the following. (Note that relevant information from the entire passage is included below, in the order it is encountered in the text, for convenience. However, the information should be entered only after it has been encountered in the passage.)

▶ What other animals are found in the marine monuments? [*Right There or Think & Search: crabs, tube worms, mussels mentioned in the "Hot Spot" section; corals, reef sharks mentioned in later sections*]

▶ What studies are scientists conducting in the marine monuments? [*Think & Search: studies of geothermal activity, including discovery of the first pool of liquid sulfur found on earth; studies of ecosystems, such as those near underwater volcanoes or involving coral reefs and schools of fish*]

▶ What is a hot spot? [*Think & Search: area of geothermal activity where magma is rising to the surface, producing an arc of volcanoes*]

▶ Can visitors go to the marine monuments? [*Right There: Answer found later in the article under the heading Tropical Treasures: Yes, but permission is needed to explore or fish there*]

Distribute a copy of the passage to each student. Ask students to read "Hot Spot" along with you or to listen carefully for information that will help you answer the questions on the class chart. Enter the QAR in the chart, along with information that answers the question. At this point, no answer information should be written if you include the question about visitors, because that information occurs in a later section of the text.

QAR	MY QUESTIONS	MY ANSWERS
BEFORE-READING QUESTIONS		
Right There	other animals in marine monuments?	crabs, tube worms, mussels
Think & Search	studies scientists conducting?	geothermal activity, ecosystems
Think & Search	hot spot?	area where magma rises to surface, forming arc of volcanoes
	visitors?	

Step 4 COACHING

Tell students that they will be working with partners to create two or three additional questions to focus their reading of the next section of text, then enter these questions in their individual charts. Give each student a blank copy of the QAR Reading Cycle Chart and have everyone enter the original questions listed on the class chart. Let students know that their questions should have something to do with the information in the heading, "Tropical Treasures" (e.g., <u>What kind of tropical treasures are found in the marine monuments?</u>). Ask students to write neatly because pairs will be exchanging their individual papers with one another.

Sample QARs, questions, and answers relevant to this section include, but aren't limited to, the following:

▶ What kind of tropical treasures are found in the marine monuments? [*Author & Me or Think & Search: The text does not spell out what tropical treasures are, so readers will probably use inference to make this determination. Tropical treasures could include living organisms, such as coral and fish, and natural resources, such as minerals, oil, and natural gas.*]

▶ What can be done to stop people from damaging the ecosystems when they're looking for tropical treasures? [*Think & Search or Right There: Information is spread across two adjacent sentences: Visitors need permission to explore or fish; commercial fishing, mining, oil and natural gas drilling within 50 miles are off-limits.*]

▶ How could the tropical treasures be used to help people? [*Author & Me: Answers will vary depending on how students have defined tropical treasures.*]

When partners have finished this task, ask them to exchange their charts with another pair (each member of the pair exchanges chart/questions with a member of the other pair) and use that pair's questions to guide their reading. Have them enter the answers they were able to locate on the QAR Reading Cycle Chart and indicate the QAR they used in answering.

Encourage partners to briefly discuss new questions they can add to the class chart. Let a few pairs share questions they found helpful in supporting their text understanding, indicating the QAR and the useful information from the text. Use students' additional questions to underscore the importance of Think & Search and Author & Me questions, and the limited information one gathers when answering Right There questions. Emphasize that valuable Right There QARs are those that focus on critically important information.

Step 5 INDEPENDENT APPLICATION

Have partners return their classmates' copies of the QAR Reading Cycle Chart. Then tell students that they will be working on their own to create questions to guide their reading of the final section of text. Refer to the last heading, "Saving Our Seas," and the QAR and the Reading Cycle Poster. Remind students that during reading, questions are usually Author & Me, Think & Search, and Right There. After reading, questions are Author & Me.

> *Based on what we have learned about the marine monuments so far, think about the kinds of questions that it would be helpful to ask next, given that the heading is "Saving Our Seas." Start by creating one during-reading question that you think would be useful in focusing your attention on the content that is signaled by this heading. Then, when you have finished reading the passage, create two after-reading questions that we can use in our closing discussion to make text-to-world and text-to-self connections. You will be sharing your work with another student, so please write neatly.*

| BEFORE READING | DURING READING | **AFTER READING** |

Have students exchange their questions with a partner. Give them time to work with the original questions from the class chart, as well as the new ones they and their partner generated that may not yet have answers. They should enter any useful new information in the third column of the QAR Reading Cycle Chart. Bring students together to share a few after-reading questions, QARs, and answers.

Step 6 SELF-ASSESSMENT & GOAL SETTING

Display the I Can Statement and ask students to keep it in mind as they discuss what they learned in today's lesson. Focus them on the ways in which questioning helps readers' understanding and how they used the title, headings, and their own interests to create questions to guide their reading of this informational text. After several students have shared their ideas, summarize by reminding them that asking appropriate questions before, during, and after reading will help them better comprehend and enjoy the text.

Close by asking students to complete the QAR Self-Assessment Thinksheet and turn it in with their finished QAR Reading Cycle Chart.

You may wish to extend this lesson to give students further practice with summarizing informational text, as taught in Lesson 10. In that case, have students use their QAR Reading Cycle Chart in place of the Important Information Chart.

Protected Paradise

By Cody Crane

The creation of three new marine monuments has turned a huge swath of Pacific Ocean into a safe haven for sea life. In a remote part of the Pacific Ocean, you can find the deepest spot on Earth, pristine coral reefs, and erupting underwater volcanoes. Millions of nesting seabirds, giant coconut crabs, rarely seen beaked whales, and endangered green sea turtles all call these waters home. It's an ocean oasis like no other in the world.

During his last days in office, former President George W. Bush announced plans to protect these unique species and geological formations for generations to come by creating three separate marine preserves. The Mariana Trench, Pacific Remote Islands, and Rose Atoll Marine National Monuments together will span 505,773 square kilometers (195,280 square miles) of ocean—an area larger than California. Their designation as monuments is one of the largest steps toward ocean conservation in history.

Hot Spot

Reaching the Mariana Trench takes researchers 15 days by boat from Hawaii. The trek to the far-flung spot is worth it. There, scientists get to study the bubbling cauldron of geothermal activity—fueled by the heat of Earth's interior—deep below the ocean's surface.

The Mariana Trench lies on the boundary between two tectonic plates (slowly moving, giant rock slabs that make up Earth's outer shell). One of the plates is slowly sliding beneath the other, forming what is called a subduction zone. The movement has created the world's deepest canyon. "It's so deep, you could put Mount Everest inside and still have a mile of ocean above," says Matt Rand, a manager at the Pew Charitable Trusts, a nonprofit group that advised the White House on the formation of the Mariana Trench Marine Monument.

As the plate along the subduction zone sinks, magma (molten rock) rises to the surface. That has produced an arc of volcanoes spread over a distance five times longer than the Grand Canyon. The tops of the volcanoes above the water have formed a chain of islands, three of which are part of the new monument.

On the slope of one underwater volcano, scientists guiding a deep-sea robot have encountered a pool of liquid sulfur—one of the first found on our planet. Prior to this discovery, a similar feature had been seen only on Jupiter's volcanic moon Io. Another

find made in these waters: a gurgling mud volcano that is 50 km (31 mi) wide. The location also harbors some of the world's largest hydrothermal vents, which spew water superheated by volcanic activity.

In spite of these harsh conditions, scientists have found thriving ecosystems (systems of interaction between living and nonliving things). Crabs, tube worms, and mussels crowd around the saunalike vents, getting their nutrients from microbes that convert chemicals from the mineral-rich waters into food.

Tropical Treasures

For use with Step 4: Coaching:

"Tropical Treasures" section

Thousands of miles to the east of the Mariana Trench sit the Remote Pacific Islands and Rose Atoll. Most of the seven Remote Islands and tiny Rose Atoll are little more than barren strips of exposed coral reef, but below the surface the coral communities bustle with life.

Here, corals blanket the ocean bottom and teem with schools of vibrantly colored fish. "I've been on dives where there were so many fish, they practically obscured my vision," says Rusty Brainard, chief of the National Oceanic and Atmospheric Administration's Coral Reef Ecosystem Division. These reefs are among the few places where sharks and other large predators (animals that kill and eat other animals) still rule the waters.

In many coastal systems and reefs, shipping, polluting, and over-fishing have wreaked havoc on sea life. Because of their isolation, the new monuments have remained largely untouched by humans. Even so, their nearness to the highly populated islands of Saipan and Guam had some researchers concerned that they could suffer a similar fate as other parts of the ocean. To help keep these areas as unspoiled as possible, visitors will now need permission to explore the monuments or to fish recreationally. Commercial fishing, mining, and oil and natural gas drilling within 80 km (50 mi) of the sites are off-limits.

Protecting the monuments will be good news not only for sea life, but also for scientists who want to study healthy marine ecosystems. "Understanding how these ecosystems are supposed to work will help us better manage other areas around the planet that are being compromised," says Brainard.

Saving Our Seas

For use with Step 5: Independent Application:

"Saving Our Seas" section

Although most Americans will never get to snorkel in a volcanic lagoon or swim with a multitude of reef sharks, their actions can still influence the future of these distant places. That's because people are affecting oceans not just locally, but on a worldwide scale.

Burning coal, oil, and natural gas for fuel generates carbon dioxide (CO_2), a heat-trapping greenhouse gas. A buildup of CO_2 in the atmosphere contributes to a rise in Earth's average temperature, known as global warming. On top of heating up, oceans absorb CO_2 and become increasingly acidic as a result. Together, these changes could cause massive die-offs of organisms that produce hard external skeletons, such as corals.

"By protecting these three huge areas, the United States is saying to the world they believe the ocean is crucial to our future," says Verena Tunnicliffe, a marine biologist at the University of Victoria in British Columbia, Canada. This move comes in addition to the creation of another marine-preservation area called Papah naumoku kea (pah-pah-HA-now-MO-koo-ah-kee-ah) Marine National Monument, created by President Bush in 2009. With these combined monuments, the U.S. will have safeguarded more of the ocean than any other country has. Still, with less than .01 percent of Earth's seas set aside as marine reserves, a lot of ocean remains in need of protecting.

Questioning With Narrative Text

GOAL ● Help students understand how to generate and respond to questions appropriate to each phase of the reading cycle

I Can Statement

I can generate and answer appropriate questions before, during, and after reading.

Reading Cycle and QARs

Reading Cycle: Before, During, and After Reading

QARs: *Right There:* Identifying important information
Think & Search: Connecting ideas across text
Author & Me: Making text-to-self connections
On My Own: Brainstorming prior to reading

Materials *(See CD for reproducibles.)*

▶ "The Adventure of the Speckled Band" adapted from the classic story by Arthur Conan Doyle (narrative passage), p. 110 (display copy, one copy for each student)

▶ The Core QARs Poster and QAR and the Reading Cycle Poster (display copy of each)

▶ QAR Reading Cycle Chart (display copy, one copy for each student)

▶ QAR Self-Assessment Thinksheet (one copy for each student)

BEFORE READING   DURING READING   AFTER READING

Step 1 EXPLICIT EXPLANATION

Remind students that they encounter questions everywhere—at home as well as at school. If students participated in Lesson 13, let them know that they will extend what they have learned about generating questions to the reading of a story or narrative text.

> *As students, you often are answering questions generated by others. The focus of today's lesson will be on reversing this situation, so that you are generating questions, not just answering them. Thinking of appropriate questions helps readers gain a deeper understanding of the text. Active readers improve their comprehension by asking questions throughout the reading cycle—before, during, and after reading.*

Step **2** MODELING

Display the QAR Reading Cycle Chart.

Note: We recommend completing Lesson 4 before this lesson. Then you can begin by reminding students to think about what they have learned about QARs and the reading cycle.

Inform students that you will be demonstrating how to use the QAR Reading Cycle Chart to keep track of: (1) the questions generated for each phase of the reading cycle, (2) the QAR likely to be most helpful in answering the question, and (3) the information that will contribute to a good answer for the question.

Display the QAR and the Reading Cycle Poster. Remind students that when we ask questions to support our comprehension, we use different QARs during each phase of the reading cycle. Have students explain why certain QARs, as identified in the poster, make sense during each phase of the reading cycle. Guide them to recall the connection of each cycle to QARs: generating background knowledge and prediction (On My Own/Author & Me) before reading, using text information and making connections during reading (Right There, Think & Search, Author & Me), and reflecting on their connections to the text and the influence of the text on their thinking after reading (Author & Me).

> *Before reading a new text or text section, questions help us think of information already in our minds that might help us understand the text and make predictions about upcoming events or information. During-reading questions help us identify important information, make connections among ideas in the text, and draw appropriate inferences. After-reading questions help us review and summarize what we just read, as well as reflect on the theme or author's message and lessons that might apply to our own lives. As you can see, questions can improve our comprehension throughout the reading cycle.*

> *Before reading, active readers ask themselves what they already know about this type of text, so they have an idea of what to expect from it. We will be reading a narrative text, so On My Own I know that it's likely to have all the elements of a story: characters, setting, problem, solution, and perhaps a theme.*

> *Before reading, I'll also think On My Own about the words in the title of the passage, "The Adventure of the Speckled Band." Hmm, the title sounds like a rock group on a road trip. It could be that, or something completely different. I'm intrigued enough to read on.*

Read the introduction aloud: "Sherlock Holmes takes on his scariest case. Adapted from Sir Arthur Conan Doyle's classic story."

> *Okay, it's definitely not about a rock group! Now that I have a bit more information, I can ask myself an Author & Me QAR. My question is, "<u>Why is this supposed to be Sherlock Holmes' scariest case?</u>"*

> *I'll use the QAR Reading Cycle Chart to organize my questions and keep track of my answers.*

In the Before-Reading Questions section of the chart, enter the QAR and question.

QAR Reading Cycle Chart

QAR	MY QUESTIONS	MY ANSWERS
BEFORE-READING QUESTIONS		
Author & Me	Why scariest case?	

Note: This lesson models note-taking to save time, but you can write the full question and answer if you believe students need to see that modeled.

DURING READING

Ask students to listen carefully as you read the first part of the text. Tell students that they should be using this information to help them think of questions to ask about the next part of the story.

Step 3 GUIDED PRACTICE

Refer to the QAR and the Reading Cycle Poster and remind students that during-reading questions are usually Author & Me, Think & Search, and Right There.

Elicit questions about the next part of the text from students, discussing the QARs that each question represents, then adding the questions to the During-Reading section of the QAR Reading Cycle Chart.

Note: Enter only the questions in the QAR Reading Cycle Chart now. The QAR is determined as you read with the questions in mind. Enter the answer after reading each section.

Sample questions and QARs are in the chart below.

QAR	MY QUESTIONS	MY ANSWERS
DURING-READING QUESTIONS		
Think & Search	Helen Toner: why frightened?	heard low whistle, same sound night sister died
Think & Search	problem or mystery?	What killed sister? Speckled band? Low whistle?
Right There (or Think & Search)	kind of person: Dr. Roylott?	strange person, no friends, two odd pets

Note: For the third question, the choice of QAR depends on students' ideas about whether the three sentences with the information qualify as being from the same place: "strange person," "no friends," "two odd pets."

Distribute a copy of the passage to each student. Ask students to read the next section along with you and listen carefully for information that will help you answer the questions on the chart. Enter the QAR in the chart, along with information that answers each question.

Step **4** COACHING

Give a blank copy of the QAR Reading Cycle Chart to each student, or have everyone draw a chart on a sheet of paper. Tell students that they will be working with partners to create two or three new questions to focus their reading of the next section of text. Ask them to add the questions already listed on the class chart to their individual chart. Explain that after they discuss possible questions, each student should then enter the new questions on their individual charts. Remind students to write neatly because they will be exchanging charts with a partner.

Sample QARs, questions, and answers relevant to this section include, but aren't limited to, the following:

▶ How could Helen's sister have been killed if her door was locked? [*Author & Me or Think & Search: Information needed to answer this question appears in the last section. However, students may be able to make some inferences about what happened, based on the clues provided by the bell pull and the ventilator. As indicated in the last section, Helen's sister died from being bitten by a speckled band, a poisonous snake from India. Dr. Roylott, the stepfather, kept the snake in his room and pushed it through the ventilator into Helen's sister's room to kill her. Then he blew a whistle to call the snake back into his room, where no one would see it.*]

▶ What caused the low whistle and the loud metal clang? [*Author & Me: Some students may be able to infer that the sound was made by the ventilator, although this information is not stated in the text. No information about the low whistle is provided in this section; the last section of the text indicates that Dr. Roylott blew a whistle to call the snake back to his room.*]

▶ What did Helen's sister mean when she said, "It was the speckled band!"? [*Think & Search: Information needed to answer this question appears in the last section. Helen's sister meant that she had been bitten by a poisonous snake called a speckled band.*]

Have partners exchange their charts with another pair so that each person has a chart from the other pair. They should then use the other pair's questions to guide their reading. Tell them to enter the answers they were able to locate on the QAR Reading Cycle Chart and indicate the QAR they used in answering the questions. Let students know that they may not find the information to answer all the questions in this section of the text.

Ask partners to briefly discuss new questions they can add to the class chart. Let a few pairs share questions they found helpful in supporting their comprehension of the text, indicating the QAR and useful text information. Use students' additional questions to underscore the importance of Think & Search and Author & Me questions during reading. Three key ideas are important to emphasize. First, in working to answer the question about how Helen's sister could have been killed when the door was locked, readers need to attend to important information and the sequence of events in the story, and use that information to draw a conclusion. This reflects high levels of thinking and use of evidence from the text, which is key to the reading process. Second, Right There QARs require readers to recognize information but not to link it together. Third, On My Own QARs do not require the use of evidence from the text to support a conclusion.

Step 5 INDEPENDENT APPLICATION

Have partners return their classmates' copies of the QAR Reading Cycle Chart. Then tell students that they will be working on their own to generate questions to guide their reading of the final section of text. Remind them that during-reading questions are usually Author & Me, Think & Search, and Right There. After-reading questions are Author & Me.

> *Based on what you have read so far, think about questions to guide your reading of the last section of the text. Start by creating a new during-reading question you think would be useful in focusing your attention as the mystery finally gets solved. Then, when you have finished reading the passage, create one after-reading question we can use in our closing discussion to make connections: text-to-text, text-to-world, and text-to-self. You will be sharing your work with another student, so please write neatly.*

Possible during-reading questions:

▶ What role might the ventilator and bell pull play in solving the mystery? [*Think & Search: because the ventilator and the bell pull were connected to the two rooms, the snake from Dr. Roylott's room could be sent into the adjacent bedroom to poison the person sleeping there. The bell pull wasn't real, but it served as a way for the snake to slither into the room unnoticed.*]

Possible questions for after reading:

▶ Why did Dr. Roylott keep a whistle and a whip near the safe? [*Author & Me: whistle to control the snake's movement and whip to protect himself if the snake returned*]

▶ Why didn't Dr. Roylott defend himself against the snake with his whip? [*Author & Me: was probably surprised, because he didn't expect the snake to return until after it killed his stepdaughter.*]

Have students exchange their questions with a partner. Give them time to work with the questions generated during Step 2, as well as any other questions they or their partners generated that have not yet been answered. They should enter any useful new information in the third column of the partner's QAR Reading Cycle Chart. Bring students together to share a few after-reading questions, their QARs, and answers.

Step **6** SELF-ASSESSMENT & GOAL SETTING

Display the I Can Statement and ask students to keep it in mind as they discuss what they learned in today's lesson. Guide them to discuss how questioning helps readers' understanding by focusing their attention on important points. Encourage students to explain how they generated questions using In My Head knowledge, such as information about mysteries, as well as In the Book or text ideas. After several students have shared their thoughts, summarize by reminding them that asking appropriate questions before, during, and after reading is a valuable strategy for promoting their understanding and enjoyment of a narrative.

Close by asking students to complete the QAR Self-Assessment Thinksheet and turn it in with their finished QAR Reading Cycle Chart.

The Adventure of the Speckled Band

Sherlock Holmes takes on his scariest case.
Adapted from Sir Arthur Conan Doyle's classic story.

For use with Step 2: Modeling:
title, first 5 paragraphs

My name is Dr. Watson. I share rooms with my friend, Sherlock Holmes. He's the most respected detective in England.

One dark night, a frightened woman knocked on our door. Her face was young, but her hair had streaks of white.

"Come in," said Holmes.

"My name is Helen Toner," she began. "I live alone with my stepfather, Dr. Roylott. He married my mother when we were living in India. Along with my sister, we moved back to England. Then, my mother died six years ago."

"Go on," said Holmes.

For use with Step 3: Guided Practice:
next 8 paragraphs

"Soon, my stepfather became strange. Now, he has no friends. He only has two odd pets, a cheetah and a baboon."

"Where is your sister?" asked Holmes.

"She died two years ago."

"Tell me the details," said Holmes.

"There are only three bedrooms in the manor," Ms. Toner began. "One for my stepfather, and one for each of us girls. The rooms open out into the same hallway. My sister and I lock our doors at night.

"One horrible night, I heard a wild scream. Then, there was a low whistle, and a loud metal clang. I ran to my sister's door, and she stumbled out. 'It was the speckled band!' she shouted, falling to the floor. No one knows how she died."

"Two days ago some repairs were started in my bedroom. I had to move into my sister's room. Last night, I again heard a low whistle. I ran from my room and took the first train to come to you."

"Very wise," said Holmes. "Can we get into the manor today without anyone knowing?"

"Yes. My stepfather is planning to be out all day."

For use with Step 4: Coaching:
next 9 paragraphs

Later that day, we met Helen at the manor. She showed us the room that had been her sister's. It had ordinary furniture.

There was an odd bell pull hanging from the ceiling, next to a ventilator. Holmes tugged at the bell pull. Nothing happened.

"Why, it's a dummy!" he said. "It is fastened to a hook just above the ventilator."

Holmes continued to examine the room. "The ventilator is also strange. It opens into the next room, rather than to the outside!"

"The ventilator and the bell pull were both built at the same time," said Helen.

Next, Holmes examined Helen's stepfather's room. There was a large metal safe. Upon it lay a leather whip.

Holmes turned to Ms. Toner. "Watson and I will stay the night in your new room. We'll see what happens."

That night, Holmes and I sat quietly for hours in the dark room. He told me that he suspected that Helen's stepfather was after the family fortune.

Soon, we heard a low whistle.

Quickly, Holmes struck a match, and beat with his cane at the bell pull.

"You see it, Watson?" he yelled. Then, a loud shriek sounded.

In the next room, we found Dr. Roylott, chin up, staring at the ceiling. The whip and a whistle lay in his lap. Round his brow he had a yellow-and-brown speckled band.

"It's the speckled band!" whispered Holmes. "It's the most poisonous snake in India. He called it with that whistle."

The snake began to move. Holmes took the whip from the dead man's lap, and grabbed the snake with it. He threw the hissing reptile into the safe, and closed the door on it.

"It appears that when I struck the snake, it returned and killed its master," said Holmes.

Such are the facts of Dr. Roylott's death. We explained them to Ms. Toner. She was relieved to have escaped her own murder.

For use with Step 5: Independent Application:
remainder of story

Monitoring Comprehension of Informational Text

GOAL • Help students monitor their comprehension and use strategies to address comprehension problems

I Can Statement

I can monitor my comprehension during reading and use QAR knowledge and tools to help me fix comprehension problems.

Reading Cycle and QARs

Reading Cycle: During Reading
QARs: *Right There:* Underscore important details
Think & Search: Locate and organize information
Author & Me: Make predictions and draw inferences to support comprehension

Materials *(See CD for reproducibles of all materials.)*

▶ "Coffee = Cash" by Libby Tucker (informational passage), p. 120 (display copy, one copy for each student)

▶ The Core QARs Poster and QAR and the Reading Cycle Poster (display copy of each)

▶ QAR Monitoring Chart (display copy, one copy for each student)

▶ QAR Fix-Up Strategies Poster (display copy)

▶ QAR Self-Assessment Thinksheet (one copy for each student)

Step **1** EXPLICIT EXPLANATION

Introduce the lesson by explaining monitoring and why it's important. Lead students to understand that monitoring enables them to do the following:

▶ Check to see that they are comprehending the text

▶ Recognize when there is a comprehension problem

▶ Use an appropriate strategy from their toolkit to address the problem

Note: This lesson uses an "inconsiderate text." This term is used to connote the problem texts students too often encounter in textbooks. Such texts, like the one used in this lesson, are confusing, may lack a clear purpose, and may be oddly or inappropriately structured. They also may include distracting information. Inconsiderate texts are useful for practicing comprehension monitoring as even highly skilled readers may find them confusing and may need to employ comprehension strategies to make sense of them.

Today I will be teaching you about monitoring, an important comprehension strategy that is used during reading. When I'm monitoring my comprehension, I'm checking to be sure that I'm maintaining a clear understanding of the text.

When I read and all the ideas in the text make sense, I experience what can be called the "click" of comprehension: My reading just clicks along! My reading is going well, and I have a good understanding of the text. In that situation, I don't really think about strategies or slow down my reading to use a particular tool that I know about— I just keep reading.

However, every now and then, I have a different experience. My reading isn't clicking along. Instead, it's more like a big comprehension "clunk." Something in the text is creating a comprehension problem for me, and my understanding breaks down. When I recognize that I've run into a problem with comprehension, a clunk, I need to do something to address the problem so I can get my comprehension clicking again.

Often, all I have to do to fix the problem is to keep reading. This is a useful strategy when the author has put a question in our minds. If we keep reading, we often find that the author gives us an answer to this question later in the text.

Sometimes I can fix the problem by going back and rereading a section. My comprehension might have broken down because I just skipped something or read something wrong. Rereading gets my comprehension back on track.

But other times, I realize that I have to do more than just continuing to read or slowing down and rereading. When this happens, I use one or more of these QAR tools we've been learning about (refer to the QAR Fix-Up Strategies Poster).

Ask students to think about the QAR tools they have learned about in previous lessons (e.g., QAR Think & Search Important Information Chart, QAR Author & Me Inference Chart, QAR and the Reading Cycle Poster). Lead a discussion of how these tools helped them comprehend text during the lessons, and the ways in which they used the tools in other situations in or out of school.

Display the QAR Monitoring Chart. Explain to students that using this chart can help them monitor comprehension during reading and choose, then use, appropriate tools to fix comprehension problems that may occur.

> *When I run into a comprehension problem—or clunk—I'll enter it in the Possible Comprehension Problem column of our QAR Monitoring Chart so I can keep the problem in mind. In the Question and QAR column, I'll write a guiding question and the possible QAR it represents so I can think about which source of information might be the most relevant to solving my comprehension clunk. To fill in the Tool to Fix the Problem column, I'll think of a QAR tool, such as those we just discussed, to help me fix the problem. I can always decide that the tool is to keep on reading, but I like having other options in case continuing to read doesn't fix the problem. In the Answer to Question column, I'll write the answer to my question. Taking these steps will help me fix my comprehension problem, so I can continue reading. Today, we'll practice this strategy with the informational passage, "Coffee = Cash."*

DURING READING

Step **2** MODELING

Display the passage. As you proceed through the text, use the coding conventions introduced in Lessons 9 and 11.

> *I'll build on the QAR coding system we used to determine important information. For monitoring, I'll use an exclamation point for information I think is important, a question mark for information that might be important, and a new code, three question marks, to indicate where I need to think more deeply before I can understand the text. I'll write the information I code with three question marks on our QAR Monitoring Chart.*

> *The title of this passage is "Coffee = Cash." I'll put three question marks next to it because I have some thinking to do about what this title means. I figure the passage is about converting coffee into cash, but since you can't literally do that, I'm not sure how that will happen. I can use an Author & Me Prediction Chart as a fix-up tool. (Write the information in the chart, as shown below.)*

> *My guiding question is, "How does coffee become cash?" I think the QAR is Author & Me and that I'll use author clues to identify useful background knowledge I have about coffee and about how money is made. (Write the information in the chart as shown below.) I don't have to create a separate QAR Author & Me Prediction Chart. Instead, I can just make some notes using the categories I remember from that chart: Author, Me, Prediction. (Write that information in the chart as shown below).*

QAR Monitoring Chart

	POSSIBLE COMPREHENSION PROBLEM	QUESTION AND QAR	TOOL TO FIX THE PROBLEM	ANSWER TO QUESTION
Section 1:		• How is coffee getting converted to cash? (Author & Me)	Author & Me Prediction Chart: • Author: coffee and cash are equal • Me: Coffee isn't money, but people can make money from selling coffee. • Prediction: I think this article will be about how students learn to make money from working in a place that sells coffee.	

Tell students that you don't know the answer to your question yet, so you can't write anything in the last column. You will keep reading to see if your prediction is correct.

Read the first two paragraphs aloud and code the information as students follow along. Potential sites for coding include the following:

Important (!): The Nest is a café in a high school. Students sell coffee and snacks.

Might be important (?): Employees aren't paid. They learn math and get experience for working outside school.

Not clear (???): (Note that everything makes sense so far.)

> *My first question already is answered, because I know that coffee becomes cash when students in this high school sell it during breakfast and lunch periods. I'm going to keep reading and coding. This section is called "Going Pro," and I see that it is sort of like a list of different categories of information. I know that a pro is a professional, like a basketball pro or a golf pro, and professionals get paid. I don't know why this list is here since the passage already told me that the students don't get paid. The title said this is about turning coffee into cash, but even with this list, I'm not clear on whether turning coffee into cash is about students' making money since they aren't paid or about the school getting money. (As you read, code each item in the list with an exclamation point: job, money, skills, get started.) "How to Get Started" feels like it is more about students, so I'm going to put three question marks next to it. This should be a Think & Search QAR, but I'm not clear which information I'll want to use.*

Make the following entries in the class chart, then continue to think aloud.

	POSSIBLE COMPREHENSION PROBLEM	QUESTION AND QAR	TOOL TO FIX THE PROBLEM	ANSWER TO QUESTION
	• purpose of the list • cash for students or cash for school	• When coffee becomes cash, who is the cash supporting? (Think & Search or Right There)	Important Information Chart: ! • Coffee becomes cash when it's sold. • Students gain experience but don't get paid in cash. ? • can earn money working in coffee shops • jobs include servers and managers • need to do math in head	

I think a useful tool is the Important Information Chart because there are a lot of details for me to keep track of and they may shift in importance.

Enter "Important Information Chart" in the Tool to Fix the Problem column, followed by the coding symbols and space to add ideas (!, ?). Add relevant ideas such as the samples in the above chart.

Conclude by revisiting the question and suggest, that at this point, you think the list might be there to help readers understand how students who volunteer in a coffee shop could turn the experience into cash—maybe by getting a paying job in a coffee café.

Step 3 GUIDED PRACTICE

Distribute a copy of the QAR Monitoring Chart to each student and a copy of the text.

Follow along or read the next section of text with me. As we read, I want you to code the information using the three symbols. The ones we code with three question marks will help us decide on our monitoring tools. (Review the three coding symbols. Emphasize that information coded ??? can be entered on the class QAR Monitoring Chart.)

As you read, pause after each phrase or sentence to give students a chance to code the text. When you have finished reading this section, briefly discuss with students the information they coded with an exclamation point or question mark. Have them give reasons for their choices. Then discuss the information students coded with three question marks. The sample chart entry below is based on a possible comprehension clunk by the sudden appearance of a money math problem in the middle of the article, similar to the appearance of the "Going Pro" section in the middle of a description of the school coffee café.

Everything I'm reading makes sense in terms of the ideas, but I'm a little confused about why this math problem is suddenly in the passage. The text tells me to answer the question to see how money math is used in a business. I know from working with math word problems that I'll need to read carefully to make sure I have the information needed to solve the problem.

	POSSIBLE COMPREHENSION PROBLEM	QUESTION AND QAR	TOOL TO FIX THE PROBLEM	ANSWER TO QUESTION
Section 2: Question 1	• Money math problem suddenly appears.	• Why is the author including a money math problem in this passage? • Will I need to solve the problem to understand the passage?	Tool 1: Solve the problem using Author & Me Inference Chart to identify what students at the Nest are learning. • Author: Smith's charges $3.98/ dozen; need to make profit • Me: 1 dozen = 12; profit = more income than expenses Inference: a. Total cost: $4 \times 12 \times 3.98 =$ $15.92 b. Sales have to be more than $15.92: $1.00 each means 16 to sell.	

I know from solving the problem that the QAR Author & Me Inference Chart is useful for keeping track of author information and what I need to add to solve the problems. I thought it was odd to find math problems in this text, but now I'm guessing that the author included these problems so I would see how important math is to the students who work at The Nest. I've learned that they definitely need to know multiplication!

Step 4 COACHING

Give each student a blank copy of the QAR Monitoring Chart.

> *You and a partner will read Problems 2 and 3 in the passage together and code the information as we have been doing. Notice that this section and the last one are math problems, which makes me think that the author is writing about students learning math by selling coffee, not about how to turn coffee into cash. As you work together, use the coding system to note important, possibly important, and potentially challenging parts of the text.*

> *When you and your partner have finished coding, use the QAR Monitoring Chart to help you think more deeply about the ideas you coded with three question marks. Enter a guiding question, its potential QAR, and the tool that will help you understand key ideas and solve the math problem.*

Give partners time to read questions 2 and 3, discuss possible comprehension problems, and tools they can use (e.g., Important Information Chart, Author & Me Chart). Circulate among students and provide assistance as needed.

If students tell you that they did not code any text information with three question marks, ask them to return to the text and identify a place that they think might be confusing to other readers, even if it was not confusing to them. A sample chart entry for this section appears below.

	POSSIBLE COMPREHENSION PROBLEM	QUESTION AND QAR	TOOL TO FIX THE PROBLEM	ANSWER TO QUESTION
Section 3: Question 2	• determining how much the wholesale price offered by Zulu saves them	• how much less profit if students had to pay Zulu's full price? (Author & Me)	Author & Me Chart: • Author: wholesale price: $4.99 per dozen; regular price: $10.99 per dozen • Me: Divide $4.99 by 12 and $10.99 by 12; round to get individual prices. Subtract: $4.99/12 from $1.00 to get profit. Take answer and subtract each from $1.00. Compare for difference in profit.	a. $.42/bagel ($4.99/dozen) b. Subtract to get profit: $1.00 – $.42 = $.58. Learned that students need to be able to divide and subtract.

▶ **Question 3:** Total cost ($1.19) requires adding individual ingredients, then selling for more ($1.20 or more) for a profit. Further money math knowledge is addition.

Have two pairs form a square of 4 students. Ask squares to compare and contrast their comprehension clunks, questions and QARs, tools for handling the problem, and their answers. Circulate among students, helping and identifying two or three pairs who have done a good job with the task.

Bring the whole class together. Call on pairs to share their charts and thinking. Elicit the idea that careful reading and rereading are essential for identifying the important information needed to solve math word problems. Help students see that the author wanted to show the kind of money math knowledge needed for success in café work. You may collect partners' work to informally evaluate the class's progress, and then use the individual work from Step 5 to evaluate individual student learning.

Step 5 INDEPENDENT APPLICATION

Tell students that they will now read the final section of the passage, two final word problems. They should code the information in the text, and then enter their questions and QARs, and comprehension tool(s) they will use to help them answer their questions in their chart. Complete the story problems, identifying information that students who work in the café need to know. Here is a sample entry for this section of the text.

	POSSIBLE COMPREHENSION PROBLEM	QUESTION AND QAR	TOOL TO FIX THE PROBLEM	ANSWER TO QUESTION
Section 4: Questions 4 and 5	• Many steps to these problems!	• How many cups are spilled during breakfast so how many more have to be sold for a profit?	Question 4: Author & Me Chart: • Author: breakfast 1 hr Coffee costs $10.00/day Individual cup: $1.25 • Me: 4 cups are spilled so add 4 cups to number sold Need 8 cups to break even (8 x $1.25), so need to sell 9 for a profit, plus the 4 spilled = 13 Question 5: Important Information Chart: baking supplies: $3.00/dozen. Nest pays $3.60/dozen. Cookies sell for $.75 apiece at Nest.	Students need to know how to use multiplication, division, addition, and subtraction. They also need to think logically about when to use these operations with the information the author gives.

Move around the room and identify two or three students who are doing a good job with the task. Bring the whole class together. Call on the students you identified earlier to share their charts and their thinking. Ask several students to share their "clunks" and the tools they used to help them keep track of the information necessary to solve the math problems. Invite them to share their thoughts about why the author included these problems in "Coffee = Cash" and how students benefited even though they did not receive salaries.

BEFORE READING   DURING READING   **AFTER READING**

Step **6** SELF-ASSESSMENT & GOAL SETTING

Display the I Can Statement and ask students to keep the statement in mind as they think about what they have learned. Use students' responses to review the tools and actions useful for fixing comprehension problems (e.g., QAR Author & Me Prediction and Inference Charts, reading further, Important Information Chart).

Conclude by asking students to identify how they can use what they have learned in this lesson to other settings. Then have them complete the QAR Self-Assessment Thinksheet and turn it in with their QAR Monitoring Chart from Steps 4 and 5.

Coffee = Cash

By Libby Tucker

For use with Step 2: Modeling:

title, introduction, and "Going Pro" section

Hanging out in a coffee shop doesn't normally count as schoolwork. But it does for students who run The Nest, a café inside a classroom at Twin Falls High School in Idaho.

Here, students sell coffee and snacks during breakfast and lunch to the school's 1,500 students and teachers. But unlike other coffee shops, The Nest doesn't pay its employees. The café helps the students learn math and get ready for life in the working world. Student Chris Hamilton told us, "Now I know how to use the cash register and count money."

Going Pro

THE JOB: Coffee Shop Employee

THE MONEY: Coffee shop counter attendants (the people who serve coffee) can earn from $14,000 to $24,000 a year. A manager earns more, ranging from $29,000 to $77,000 per year.

NECESSARY SKILLS: Neat appearance and good manners; ability to remember customers' orders; quick math skills for adding prices or making change; ability to work as part of a team.

HOW TO GET STARTED: The minimum working age varies by state. Most coffee shops do not require prior experience, so to get started, just apply! They usually provide training, but the best way to learn is to observe a more experienced worker.

THE NEST'S CHRIS HAMILTON SAYS: "The cash register tells you what money to give back, but I also have to do math in my head."

For use with Step 3: Guided Practice:

next 3 paragraphs and Problem 1

The Nest needs to make enough money to cover basic expenses such as coffee beans and food, paper cups and plates, and uniforms. It also needs to have money left over to expand the menu. For example, the café just started selling Italian sodas and cookies made by the school's baking class.

"I like math; it keeps me busy," said Chelsie Tipton, who also works at The Nest. "I'll work in the coffee shop for a while, then I'll go to another job."

Answer our questions to see how The Nest uses money math to do business. After all, it may look like a café, but it's still a classroom!

1. When The Nest started selling bagels, the students bought them from Smith's Grocery Store for $3.98 per dozen. The goal is to sell the bagels for a profit.

a. If they buy 4 dozen bagels for the week, how much will that cost them?

b. If they sell the bagels for $1.00 each, how many must they sell in a week to make a profit?

For use with Step 4: Coaching:

Problems 2 and 3

2. A local shop, Zulu Bagels, offered to supply higher-quality bagels to The Nest at a wholesale price—or lower than they normally charge—of $4.99 a dozen. (Customers who buy their bagels in Zulu's shop regularly pay $10.99 a dozen.)

a. How much does each bagel cost The Nest?

b. If the students keep selling bagels for $1, how much profit will they make for each bagel they sell? (Round to the nearest penny.)

3. The students added Italian sodas to the list of drinks they sell. Given the following list of ingredients and their costs, calculate the minimum amount they should charge for each drink in order to make a profit. 16-ounce plastic cup, $0.12; plastic dome lid, $0.06; flavoring, $0.44; sparkling water, $0.10; half-and-half cream, $0.08; whipped cream, $0.38; straw, $0.01; and ice, free from the cafeteria!

For use with Step 5: Independent Application:

Problems 4 and 5

4. School starts late on Wednesday, and it is The Nest's busiest day, because breakfast is an hour (7:30 to 8:30 a.m.) instead of a half hour. Customers have more time to buy breakfast, but the cafe's employees become rushed and spill more coffee! The Nest spends $10 a day on coffee and sells it for $1.25 per cup. But let's say one cup is spilled every 15 minutes during breakfast. How many total cups must they sell to make a profit? (Hint: They'll need to sell an extra cup for each one spilled.)

5. The Nest sells chocolate chip and peanut butter cookies baked by the school's culinary arts students. Baking supplies cost that baking class $3.00 per dozen cookies. The class charges The Nest $3.60 a dozen for the cookies. The Nest sells the cookies for $0.75 each. If the baking students sold the cookies themselves at that same price, how much more profit per dozen would they make than The Nest makes?

Monitoring Comprehension of Narrative Text

GOAL • Help students monitor their comprehension and use strategies to address comprehension problems

I Can Statement

I can monitor my comprehension during reading and use QAR knowledge and tools to help me fix comprehension problems.

Reading Cycle and QARs

Reading Cycle: During Reading

QARs: *Right There:* Underscore important information
Think & Search: Locate and organize information
Author & Me: Make predictions and draw inferences to support comprehension

Materials *(See CD for reproducibles.)*

▶ "The Legend of Guanina" (narrative passage), p. 128 (display copy, one copy for each student)

▶ The Core QARs Poster and QAR and the Reading Cycle Poster (display copy of each)

▶ QAR Monitoring Chart (one copy for each student)

▶ QAR Fix-Up Strategies Poster (display copy)

▶ QAR Self-Assessment Thinksheet (one copy for each student)

Step **1** EXPLICIT EXPLANATION

If students participated in Lesson 15, make the connection to it by explaining that today's lesson continues the focus on monitoring. In this lesson, they'll be reading a narrative text. If not, tell students that they will be learning about monitoring, an important comprehension strategy that active readers use during reading. Explain that monitoring helps active readers do three things.

Note: If you have taught Lesson 15, invite students to share what they remember from the lesson about these three monitoring actions:

1. Check to see that they are comprehending the text
2. Recognize when there is a comprehension problem
3. Use an appropriate strategy from their toolkit to address the problem

Display the QAR Fix-Up Strategies Poster to review the QAR tools now in their toolkit (e.g., QAR Think & Search Important Information Chart, QAR and the Reading Cycle Poster) and the purpose of each tool. Explain that even active readers do not use all the tools all the time. Rather, active readers think about their purpose for reading, the tools they have available, and how to use a tool when they need to do so to ensure they will understand the text.

A think-aloud patterned after the one in Lesson 15 is included below. If you have taught Lesson 15, use students' performance in that lesson as the basis for determining how much of this think-aloud to repeat, modify, or skip. Key points appear in bold.

> *Today I will teach you about an important comprehension strategy that is used during reading—monitoring. Monitoring helps me decide when I need to use tools from my comprehension toolkit to help me better understand what I am reading. Monitoring helps me notice that much of the time my reading is going smoothly—I experience the "click" of comprehension. I can find information for my predictions, recognize important information, and draw inferences when I need to. In this case, I just keep reading along.*
>
> *Monitoring also helps me pay attention to comprehension problems while reading. Instead of a click, I experience a "clunk" of comprehension. I realize that the text is not making sense to me. When this happens, I need to slow down and reread. If I try rereading the text and find that it still doesn't make sense, I know that I need to go to my comprehension toolkit.*
>
> *Sometimes I've experienced a clunk because of an unfamiliar word or phrase— something that is Right There in the text that <u>should</u> help me isn't very useful. Sometimes I know all the words, but there's a lot of information to keep organized in my head. I find that I am confused or that I keep forgetting things I've just read. And sometimes I realize that while I know all the words, I don't know enough On My Own*

to make sense of what is in the text. So not all comprehension clunks occur for the same reasons.

Display the QAR Monitoring Chart (introduced in Lesson 15; make this connection if students participated in that lesson). Explain to students that using this chart can help them monitor comprehension during reading and choose and use the tools to fix comprehension problems that may occur.

> *When I run into a comprehension problem, or clunk, I can enter the problem in the Possible Comprehension Problem column of the QAR Monitoring Chart. This helps me remember what caused the clunk. In the Question and QAR column, I write the question I have and the possible QAR it represents so that I can think about which source of information might be most relevant. To fill in the Tools to Fix the Problem column, I think of a comprehension strategy tool, such as those we just discussed, to help me fix the problem. I can always decide that the tool is to keep on reading, but I like having some other options in case that doesn't fix the problem. In the Answer to the Question column, I write the answer to my question. Taking these steps helps me fix my comprehension problem so I can continue reading.*

DURING READING

Step **2** MODELING

Display the first section of the passage, "The Legend of Guanina." As you proceed through the text, use the coding conventions detailed in Lesson 15.

> *I'm going to use the QAR coding system we used in Lesson 15 to monitor my comprehension. I'll use an exclamation point for information that I think is important, a question mark for information that might be important, and three question marks to indicate where I need to think more deeply before I can understand the text. The information coded with three-question marks is what I'll enter on our QAR Monitoring Chart.*
>
> *The title of this passage is "The Legend of Guanina." A legend is a story, so this will tell the story about something or someone called Guanina, but I'm going to code Guanina with three question marks since I don't know who or what that is, and I'm pretty sure I'll need to understand this to make sense of the story.*
>
> *I have my first entry for my QAR Monitoring Chart.* (Think aloud as you enter "Guanina" in the Comprehension Problem column, followed by "Who or what is Guanina" in the next column). *The QAR is likely Right There or Think & Search because the text should tell me the answer to my question, so for now, I'm going to use the strategy of continuing to read* (enter in Tool to Fix the Problem column).

	POSSIBLE COMPREHENSION PROBLEM	QUESTION AND QAR	TOOL TO FIX THE PROBLEM	ANSWER TO QUESTION
Section: 1	• Guanina	• Who or what is Guanina? (Right There or Think & Search)	• keep reading	

Tell students that you will enter relevant information in the last column if you come across it as you continue reading. Then read the first three paragraphs aloud, coding information as students follow along. Potential sites for coding include the following:

!: Guanina—a beautiful Taino princess; Spanish arrived to get gold for Spain

?: 500 years ago, had a good life, uncle was village chief

???: Spanish conquistadores, Guanina and her uncle were friendly to the Spanish; Guanina and Don Cristobal fell in love

I've learned right away that Guanina was a princess leading a good life, so that answers my first question using Right There as my QAR. I'll keep reading and coding as I work through the rest of this section. It seems like things are going pretty well for Guanina, but right after saying that her family was happy, the author says that Spanish conquistadores came to their town. I'm going to code this with three question marks, as needing deeper thinking, for two reasons. One is that it seems like the author is warning me, contrasting the arrival of the Spanish with the villagers' happiness. Also, I know that the Spanish took over many of the islands in this part of the world. I'm also using three question marks to code the information about how friendly Guanino and her uncle were to the Spanish, and that she fell in love, because I thought the Spanish were the enemy.

Continue to model as you turn the ??? codes into QAR Monitoring Chart entries. See the sample chart entries below.

	POSSIBLE COMPREHENSION PROBLEM	QUESTION AND QAR	TOOL TO FIX THE PROBLEM	ANSWER TO QUESTION
Section: 1	• Spanish arrive in Guanina's town	• What will happen to Guanina and her village now that the Spanish have arrived?	QAR Important Information Chart: • ! – village leaders friendly to Spanish – Spanish purpose is to get gold • ? – Guanina and Don Cristobal fall in love	

Step 3 GUIDED PRACTICE

Distribute a copy of the QAR Monitoring Chart to each student along with a copy of the passage.

> *Follow along as I read aloud the next section of the passage, or read it with me. As we read, I want you to code the information using the three symbols. The ones we code with three question marks will help us determine which monitoring tools to use. (If necessary, review the three coding symbols and remind students that information coded "???" can be entered on the class QAR Monitoring Chart.)*

As you read, pause after each phrase or sentence to give students a chance to code the text. When you have finished reading this section, briefly discuss with students the information they coded with an exclamation point or question mark. Have them give reasons for their choices. Items that students are likely to find important include the following: <u>Spanish enslavement of Tainos; Guaybana becoming chief and his desire for revenge; Guanina's conflicting feelings.</u> Possibly important items could include the following: <u>uncle's death; Guaybana's plans for revenge; her warning to Don Cristobal.</u> Guide students to complete the entries in their charts for text information they coded ???. The chart below shows a sample based on the potential problem of understanding the importance of Guanina's role in the legend; the story so far seems more about her brother's plan for revenge.

	POSSIBLE COMPREHENSION PROBLEM	QUESTION AND QAR	TOOL TO FIX THE PROBLEM	ANSWER TO QUESTION
Section: 2	• Legend is about Guanina, but her brother seems to be a more important character right now.	• What does Guanina do to become the focus of the legend? (Think & Search)	Author & Me Prediction Chart: • Author: Guanina loves Don Cristobal even though he has enslaved her people. Her brother has decided to kill Don Cristobal and his men. Guanina warns Don Cristobal • Me: Brothers can be angry when sisters don't do what they want. Stars of legends are usually heroes or heroines. • Prediction: Guaybana will try to punish his sister, and she'll fight back and somehow save Don Cristobal.	

Step 4 COACHING

Give each student a blank copy of the QAR Monitoring Chart or have them draw it on a sheet of paper. Remind them to fill in the section number.

> *You and a partner will read the third section of this passage together. As you work together, use the coding system to note important, possibly important, and potentially challenging parts of the text. You should keep our prediction in mind as a way of checking to see if we are making sense of the legend and if we are identifying the important information needed to further our understanding.*

> *When you and your partner have finished coding, use your QAR Monitoring Chart to discuss the ideas you coded with three question marks. Together, decide on a useful guiding question, likely QAR, and related tool(s) you could use to address the question. In your chart, enter the guiding question you and your partner created, its likely QAR, and the tool or tools that you will use to help you understand key ideas and solve the comprehension problem.*

Give partners time to read the next five paragraphs, then discuss possible comprehension problems and tools they can use (e.g., Important Information Chart, Author & Me Prediction Chart). Circulate around the group and provide assistance as needed. If students tell you that they did not code any text information with three question marks, ask them to return to the text and identify a place that they think might be confusing to other readers, even if it was not confusing to them. A sample entry appears below.

	POSSIBLE COMPREHENSION PROBLEM	QUESTION AND QAR	TOOL TO FIX THE PROBLEM	ANSWER TO QUESTION
Section: 3	• invincible	• What does it mean to be invincible? (Think & Search or Author & Me)	QAR Identifying Important Information • doesn't take many soldiers with him • wasn't afraid • conquered the Tainos	• maybe means "brave" or maybe means "can't be beaten" • not enough context clues to be certain

Have each pair share their responses with another pair, noting similarities and differences in the potential comprehension clunks they identified and helping each other where they can. Circulate among students, assisting as necessary and identifying two or three pairs who have done a good job with the task.

Bring the whole class together and invite the pairs you identified to share their charts and thinking. Elicit that Don Cristobal was overconfident and thought he could not be beaten, giving Guaybana an advantage when he attacked the small group of Spaniards. You may collect partners' work to informally evaluate the class's progress. Use the completed work from Step 5 to evaluate individual student learning.

Step 5 INDEPENDENT APPLICATION

Tell students that they will now read the final section of the passage. They should code information, enter their questions and QARs, and the comprehension tool(s) to use to help them answer their questions. Here is a sample entry for this section of the text.

	POSSIBLE COMPREHENSION PROBLEM	QUESTION AND QAR	TOOL TO FIX THE PROBLEM	ANSWER TO QUESTION
Section: Final	• Guanina felt a sharp pain in her heart at the same time Don Cristobal died.	• Why did she have a pain if she hadn't been attacked?	• Author & Me Prediction Chart: • Author: She and Don Cristobal were in love. This passage is a legend. • Me: Legends sometimes have exaggerated events. • Prediction: Guanina has a "broken heart."	• The author wrote she died of "grief"" which is like a broken heart.

Move around the room and identify two or three students who are doing a good job with the task. Bring the whole class together. Call on the students you identified earlier to share their comprehension "clunks" and the tools they used to fix these problems.

BEFORE READING   DURING READING   **AFTER READING**

Step 6 SELF-ASSESSMENT & GOAL SETTING

Display the I Can Statement and ask students to keep it in mind as they consider what they have learned about monitoring. Use students' responses to review the tools and actions useful for fixing comprehension problems (e.g., QAR Author & Me Prediction and Inference Charts, reading further, rereading, Important Information Chart).

Ask students to identify how they can use what they have learned in other settings. Guide them to recognize that monitoring is a strategy that can improve their comprehension of all texts, ranging from math word problems to novels to Web sites. Finally, ask students to complete the QAR Self-Assessment Thinksheet and turn it in with their QAR Monitoring Chart from Steps 4 and 5.

The Legend of Guanina

For use with Step 2: Modeling:
title and first 3 paragraphs

Five centuries ago, Puerto Rico was called Borinquen (bore-in-KANE). The Taino (tah-EE-no) people lived there. Guanina (gwa-NEE-na) was a beautiful Taino princess.

Guanina had a good life. Her uncle was the chief of her village. Their family was happy.

Then, in 1508, Spanish conquistadores (con-KEES-ta-DOOR-ace) came to Borinquen. Guanina's uncle welcomed the Spanish. He even let their leader, Don Cristobal, build a house in his own village.

For use with Step 3: Guided Practice:
next 4 paragraphs

Guanina was friendly to the Spanish too. She showed them around Borinquen. As she and Don Cristobal walked together, they fell in love.

Don Cristobal was kind to Guanina. But the Spanish weren't on the island to make friends. They were there to get gold for Spain.

The Spanish enslaved the Tainos. They threatened them with swords and forced them to mine Borinquen for gold. Soon Guanina's uncle died. Her brother, Guaybana [gwy-BAH-nah], became the new chief.

Guaybana was angry with the Spanish. He wanted revenge. In 1511, he decided to kill Don Cristobal and the rest of the conquistadores.

For use with Step 4: Coaching:
next 5 paragraphs

Guanina was torn. She understood her brother's anger, but she loved Don Cristobal. She visited her lover in secret.

"Leave Borinquen," she whispered. "My brother, the chief, wants to kill you. Please save yourself."

Don Cristobal wasn't afraid. He had conquered the Tainos. He felt like he was invincible.

Soon, he had to travel to another village. He took only four Spanish soldiers with him. He ordered Guaybana to bring him servants to carry his bags.

The Taino servants arrived. They frowned at Guanina as she kissed Don Cristobal goodbye. As he left, he promised, "I will return safely, Guanina."

For use with Step 5: Independent Application:
remainder of story

When the Spanish travelers were out of sight, Guaybana put on his feathered headdress and led his best warriors on a shortcut through the forest. They caught up with the Spanish.

When Don Cristobal heard the warriors coming, he knew Guanina had been right. The battle began. Taino clubs and Spanish swords flew. Warriors from both sides were slain.

Don Cristobal was the last of the Spanish to die. He was attacking Guaybana when a Taino warrior began hitting him with a club. The pain of the blows made him drop his sword. Soon he fell dead beside it. The Tainos had won.

At the moment when Don Cristobal died, Guanina felt a sharp pain in her heart. She ran through the forest, only to find his dead body. She fell to her knees, screaming in horror.

Meanwhile, Guaybana's men were carrying their dead home to be buried. "The Spanish fought bravely," said Guaybana. "Don Cristobal deserves a proper burial. Go get his body."

When Guaybana's men returned for Don Cristobal's body, they found Guanina clinging to it. The men went back to tell Guaybana.

"She's a traitor," said Guaybana. "We'll kill her tomorrow. She'll be buried with him."

The next morning, the men returned to the spot. Guanina was lying still beside Don Cristobal's body. She had died of grief.

The two lovers were put in a single grave. On the grave, pure white lilies and deep red poppies still grow. Sometimes, in that spot, you can still hear their love songs in the wind.